SOPHOCLES' KING OIDIPOUS

SOPHOCLES' KING OIDIPOUS
TRANSLATION WITH NOTES, INTRODUCTION AND ESSAY

RUBY BLONDELL
UNIVERSITY OF WASHINGTON

Focus Classical Library
Focus Publishing
R. Pullins Company
Newburyport MA

THE FOCUS CLASSICAL LIBRARY
Series Editors • James Clauss and Stephen Esposito

Aristophanes: Acharnians • Jeffrey Henderson
Aristophanes: The Birds • Jeffrey Henderson
Aristophanes: Clouds • Jeffrey Henderson
Aristophanes: Frogs • Henderson
Aristophanes: Lysistrata • Jeffrey Henderson
Aristophanes: Three Comedies: Acharnians, Lysistrata, Clouds • Jeffrey Henderson
Euripides: The Bacchae • Stephen Esposito
Euripides: Four Plays: Medea, Hippolytus, Heracles, Bacchae • Stephen Esposito, ed.
Euripides: Hecuba • Robin Mitchell-Boyask
Euripides: Heracles • Michael R. Halleran
Euripides: Hippolytus • Michael R. Halleran
Euripides: Medea • Anthony Podlecki
Euripides: The Trojan Women • Diskin Clay
Golden Verses: Poetry of the Augustan Age • Paul T. Alessi
Golden Prose in the Age of Augustus • Paul T. Alessi
Hesiod: Theogony • Richard Caldwell
Hesiod: Theogony & Works and Days • Stephanie Nelson
The Homeric Hymns • Susan Shelmerdine
Ovid: Metamorphoses • Z. Philip Ambrose
Plautus: Captivi, Amphitryon, Casina, Pseudolus • David Christenson
Roman Comedy: Five Plays by Plautus and Terence • David Christenson
Roman Lives • Brian K. Harvey
Sophocles: Antigone • Ruby Blondell
Sophocles: Electra • Hanna M. Roisman
Sophocles: King Oidipous • Ruby Blondell
Sophocles: Oidipous at Colonus • Ruby Blondell
Sophocles: Philoktetes • Seth Schein
Sophocles: The Theban Plays • Ruby Blondell
Terence: Brothers (Adelphoe) • Charles Mercier
Vergil: The Aeneid • Richard Caldwell

Copyright © 2002 Ruby Blondell

Cover: Sommavilla Painter, calyx krater, Museo Archaelogico Nazionale di Antichita at Parma.

ISBN 13: 978-1-58510-060-6
ISBN 10: 1-58510-060-9

10 9 8 7 6 5 4 3 2

This book is published by Focus Publishing / R. Pullins Company, PO Box 369, Newburyport MA 01950. All rights are reserved. No part of this publication may be produced, stored in a retrieval system, produced on stage or otherwise performed, transmitted by any means, electronic, mechanical, by photocopying, recording, or by any other media or means without the prior written permission of the publisher.

If you have received this material as an examination copy free of charge, Focus Publishing/R. Pullins Company retains the title to the material and it may not be resold. Resale of any examination copies of Focus Publishing/R. Pullins Company materials is strictly prohibited.

0910TS

To my friends

φίλον γὰρ ἐσθλὸν ἐκβαλεῖν ἴσον λέγω
καὶ τὸν παρ᾽ αὑτῷ βίοτον, ὃν πλεῖστον φιλεῖ

Table of Contents

Preface

Sophocles' *King Oidipous* has been translated countless times. This new translation is aimed at all those, especially students and teachers, who wish to work with an English version that closely follows the Greek original. I have tried to remain reasonably faithful to Greek idiom and metaphor, to translate words important for the meaning of the play consistently, and sometimes to retain the original word order, verse and sentence structure. The original meters have inevitably been sacrificed, but I have used a kind of six-beat iambic line for the iambic (spoken) portion of the drama, and tried to retain an approximately anapestic rhythm for Sophocles' anapests (which are printed in italics). I have not used any formal metrical scheme for the lyrics, which are simply rendered in short lines and indented. (In order to avoid confusing the reader, in some lyric passages I have increased the number of lines so that they approximate more closely to the marginal line numbers, which are the same as in the Greek text.) Despite this attempt to retain some of the rhythmic sense of the original, my first priorities have usually been accuracy and consistency. This approach sometimes leads to awkward moments, but I hope they will be outweighed by its benefits. Though many aspects of the original have been lost, as they must be in any translation, I believe, and hope the reader will agree, that much of the poetry of meaning is best communicated in this way.

The spellings of Greek names attempt to retain some of the benefits of both comfort and defamiliarization. For the most part I have used traditional English spelling for the names of historical persons and places (e.g. Aeschylus, Athens), but transliterated mythological names in so far as this accords with modern English pronunciation (e.g. Kreon, Polyneices). There are further reasons for preferring Oidipous to Oedipus, since the former captures more effectively the many puns upon his name, some of which are explained in the notes and essay. The explanatory notes are aimed at those approaching this play, and perhaps ancient Greek culture, for the first time. They provide factual information on such matters as mythology, geography and unfamiliar cultural practices, together with clarification of obscure phrases and some interpretive pointers. There are no stage directions in ancient Greek texts. Those provided in the translation are based on indications in the dialogue, and are intended to clarify the stage action for the modern reader. A fuller discussion of important background material concerning the poet, his theater and the myth of Oidipous and his family is contained in the Introduction. The translation is followed by an interpretive Essay, to be read after the play, together with some suggestions for further reading.

The translation was based on the Greek of Hugh Lloyd-Jones and Nigel Wilson's Oxford Classical Text (Oxford 1990), but I have departed from their text on occasion. Most lines bracketed by these editors have been left unbracketed in order to avoid prejudging textual issues. My translation and notes are also indebted to Jebb's great work,[1] and to a lesser extent to the more recent commentaries by Dawe and Kamerbeek.[2] I am most grateful to my students, colleagues and friends who read all or parts of the manuscript and made suggestions for improvement, especially Michael Halleran, Brady Mechley, and the members of my Sophocles seminar in Fall 2001.

University of Washington

---

1 R.C.Jebb, *Sophocles, the Plays and Fragments. Part I: The Oedipus Tyrannus* (2nd edition Cambridge 1887)

2 J.C. Kamerbeek, *The Plays of Sophocles. Commentaries Part IV: The Oedipus Tyrannus* (Leiden 1967); Dawe (ed.), R.D. *Sophocles: Oedipus Rex* (Cambridge 1982).

Introduction

SOPHOCLES[1]

Of the hundreds of tragedies produced in fifth-century BCE Athens, only a handful of works by just three dramatists have survived to the present day. Seven of these plays are by the poet Sophocles, who was born at Colonus, the rural village near Athens where his play *Oidipous at Colonus* is set, in about 495 BCE. This makes him a generation younger than his great predecessor Aeschylus (c. 525-456), and ten or fifteen years older than Euripides (c. 480-406). But the relationship between the three tragedians and their works is not strictly linear. The first dozen years of Sophocles' career overlapped with Aeschylus' final years, and for the rest of his long life Euripides was his rival. Aeschylus made use of Sophocles' theatrical innovations (discussed below), and Sophocles in turn was influenced by Euripides. It is said that when Euripides died in 406 BCE, Sophocles dressed his chorus in mourning at a public ceremony which preceded the dramatic festival (the *proagōn*). He himself was to die later the same year, or early in the next. In the fourth century and beyond, these three men rapidly became canonized as the great figures of the Athenian tragic theater, which led to the survival of some of their works when the entire output of the other tragic playwrights was lost. As with all ancient texts, the survival of these particular plays depended not only on the vagaries of taste, but on the chancy process of the copying and recopying of manuscripts, until the advent of printing nearly two thousand years later.

Sophocles lived a long and active life, spanning almost the whole of the fifth century BCE, which saw a great many political and cultural achievements at Athens. We know almost nothing of his background (except that his father, Sophillus, is said to have

---

1 This introduction is adapted from the Introduction to *Sophocles' Antigone, with Introduction, Translation and Essay*, by Mary Whitlock Blundell (Focus Classical Library: Newburyport, MA 1998).

owned a weapons factory), but the evidence of his career suggests a well-connected family. Like any Athenian boy whose father could afford it, he will have received the customary education in music, poetry and athletics. The mainstay of this education was Homer, especially the *Iliad*, which was thought to embody not just literary excellence but traditional cultural and moral values. As a boy, Sophocles will have learned to recite large quantities of the epic from memory. This must have been especially significant for the future playwright whom later writers were to describe as 'most Homeric' of the tragedians.

The poet's childhood coincided with the Persian Wars, in which the Greeks, largely under the leadership of Athens, foiled repeated Persian attempts to invade the Greek mainland. Sophocles was about five years old when the Athenians won their first great victory over the Persians at the battle of Marathon (490 BCE). When the Persians were defeated again, in a sea-battle off the island of Salamis in 480 BCE, the young Sophocles is said to have led the dance in celebration of the victory. If true, this was a significant honor, as well as a tribute to the youth's good looks and physical grace. He grew to maturity in the years that followed the Persian Wars, when the power and influence of Athens were on the rise. After the war the city had founded the Delian League, an alliance of Greek states for mutual defense against the Persians. But as the fifth century progressed Athens took increasing control of the League, until it grew to resemble an Athenian empire rather than an alliance of free states. The subject allies were required to pay Athens large amounts of annual tribute in the form of ships or money. This period of Athenian history is marked by the leadership of Pericles, who was born around the same time as Sophocles and dominated public life from about 460 BCE until his death from the plague in 429. He both strengthened democracy at home and expanded Athenian influence abroad, in large part by exploiting Athenian leadership of the Delian League.

One of Pericles' most ambitious enterprises was the public building program that culminated in the construction of the Parthenon—the great temple of Athena on the Acropolis at Athens. Like other such projects, this temple, with its magnificent architecture and sculptural decoration, was partly financed by taxes from members of the Delian League. Besides supporting the visual arts, Pericles was a patron of writers and thinkers, helping to promote the extraordinary artistic and intellectual accomplishments of fifth-century Athens. Literary excellence was also fostered by the generally open and tolerant nature of the Athenian democratic ideal, which placed a high value on artistic achievement and freedom of expression. (Socrates was active as a provocative 'gadfly' throughout most of this period, and was not prosecuted until 399 BCE, after Athens had become demoralized by defeat and less tolerant of public criticism.) But the cultural achievements of Periclean Athens meant little to the oppressed members of its empire or to its rivals, headed by Sparta. In 431 BCE, when Sophocles was in his sixties, the resentment aroused by Athenian expansion culminated in the outbreak of the Peloponnesian War, between Athens with its allies on one side and Sparta with its allies on the other. This long and draining war dominated the last twenty-five years of the poet's life, and he was to die before it finally ended in the defeat of Athens in 404 BCE.

Sophocles began his dramatic career in 468 BCE with a group of four plays that have not survived. He defeated Aeschylus to win first prize in the tragic competition (on which see further below). By this time tragedy in Athens had already developed into a mature art form. But the conventions of the genre were not static, and Sophocles had a reputation in antiquity as a theatrical innovator. Aristotle tells us in his *Poetics* that he increased the number of actors from two to three, and introduced the practice of scene painting. He is also said to have enlarged the size of the chorus from twelve to fifteen, written a book on dramaturgy, and founded an artistic society dedicated to the Muses (the patron goddesses of music and the arts). In the course of his long career he wrote more than a hundred and twenty dramas—about ninety tragedies and thirty satyr plays (a kind of mythological burlesque). Of this enormous output we have only seven tragedies, significant parts of two satyr plays and some scattered fragments. The survival of these particular plays was not random, but probably results from their conscious selection as Sophocles 'best' plays, in somebody's opinion, at some point in the process of transmission.

Of the surviving tragedies we have secure production dates for only two, which also happen to be the last of the seven: *Philoctetes*, produced in 409 BCE, and *Oidipous at Colonus*, produced posthumously in 401. The dating of *Ajax*, *Electra* and *Women of Trachis* is highly speculative. *Antigone* may have been produced about 442 BCE. The evidence for this is insecure, however. An ancient commentator tells us that Sophocles was elected general for the Samian war (which began in 441) because of the admiration aroused by this play. We know from other evidence that Sophocles did indeed hold such a post, serving with Pericles during the Samian revolt of 441/440. The idea that he was elected on the strength of *Antigone* is thought by most scholars to be dubious, like many stories concerning the lives of ancient poets; but it is not impossible, given the ancient Athenians' belief in the educational value of poetry, and the explicitly political subject matter of *Antigone*. (A fourth-century orator was to quote Kreon's opening speech with approval for its patriotic content.) Even if the story is untrue, however, it was probably fabricated precisely because the play preceded the generalship rather closely. But *Antigone* could not have been produced in 441, since the election preceded the dramatic festival. So a hypothetical date, usually accepted for lack of any other evidence, is 442. *Oidipous the King* was probably produced somewhere between 430 and 425, but once again the evidence is tenuous. For example the description of the plague that opens the play is often thought to have been influenced by the terrible plague that devastated Athens at the outset of the Peloponnesian War, in which Pericles died, along with a quarter of the Athenian population. But although this *may* be true, it is scarcely conclusive, especially since there is also a tradition of literary plague-descriptions going back to the opening of Homer's *Iliad*. Accordingly, some scholars have dated the play earlier than the beginning of the war.

Whether or not we believe that *Antigone* secured Sophocles' election as general, it does suggest both the high regard in which a popular poet might be held, and the lack of a sharp dichotomy between achievement in artistic and political life. As his service as general illustrates, Sophocles took an active part in the political, military and religious life of Athens, in line with cultural expectations for male citizens of the leisured classes. An anecdote about this military campaign helps bring him to life for us. A contemporary writer reports that one day when the two men were dining together Pericles remarked that Sophocles was a good poet but a bad strategist; in response, the poet displayed his strategic expertise by stealing a kiss from a handsome boy who was pouring the wine. Another story, from Plato, recounts that Sophocles was relieved to be freed by old age from the tyranny of sexual desire for women (*Republic* 329bc). Such anecdotes suggest an urbane and passionate man who participated in the wide range of activities—political, social, erotic—expected of his gender, class and culture.

Besides serving as general, Sophocles held the important office of public treasurer in 443/2. Late in life he was again chosen for significant public office. In 413 BCE Athens suffered a crushing defeat in Sicily, and the poet (now more than eighty years old) was one of ten commissioners appointed to reorganize Athenian affairs after the crisis. Another incident shows him participating in a different area of public life. In 420 BCE the cult of Asklepios, god of medicine, was formally introduced into Athens. The god, who took the form of a snake, remained in the house of Sophocles until his official residence could be prepared. For this service the poet was honored with a cult after his death.

Sophocles was probably acquainted with many of the most important cultural figures of his day. Besides the association with Pericles, his name is connected with such people as the philosopher Archelaus (the teacher of Socrates), and the historian Herodotus. Both *Antigone* and *Oidipous at Colonus* provide evidence for his familiarity with Herodotus' work. When Oidipous compares his sons to the Egyptians, whose customs are said to be the opposite of the Greeks' (*OC* 337-41), he is probably drawing on the colorful account in the second book of Herodotus' *Histories* (2.35). And when Antigone explains that she buried her brother because, unlike a child or husband, he is irreplaceable (*Ant.* 904-12), she too is echoing an argument from Herodotus (3.119).[2]

The plays of Sophocles also show an unmistakable familiarity with the rhetorical techniques popularized by the contemporary thinkers known as 'sophists.' These itinerant intellectuals offered instruction in many subjects, and were associated with moral relativism and other intellectual challenges to traditional moral and religious values. Their principle subject, however, was rhetoric, for which they found a ready audience at Athens, where public life was pervaded by debate and persuasive speaking was the key to political success. In democratic Athens public policy was decided by an assembly open to all adult male citizens, who voted on each issue after extensive debate. Athenian society was also highly litigious, and a citizen had to plead his own case in court before a jury of several hundred of his peers. It is therefore not surprising that the dramatists and their audience had a highly developed appreciation for this kind of oratory. Though Sophocles' style may seem less self-consciously rhetorical than that of Euripides, the influence of public oratory can clearly be seen, especially in the long and formal speeches with which his characters often debate each other.

Sophocles lived to the age of about ninety. The story goes that in his advanced old age he quarreled with his son Iophon, who then sued him for senility under a law allowing a son to take control of an incompetent father's property. In his own defense, Sophocles read aloud in court from the play he was working on at the time: the opening lines of the song in praise of the Athenian land in *Oidipous*

---

2 I use the standard abbreviations *OT* (= *Oidipous Turannos*) to refer to *King Oidipous*, *Ant.* for *Antigone*, and *OC* for *Oidipous at Colonus*.

at Colonus (668-93). Naturally he was acquitted. Like most such stories, this one is unlikely to be true. (It is probably derived from a contemporary comedy, lampooning the poet and his son.) But it tells us something about the image of Sophocles that was constructed even at an early date. He did not attract such colorful anecdotes as many others, including the other two major tragedians. (Aeschylus was supposedly killed by a tortoise dropped on his head by an eagle, and Euripides was said to be a misanthropic cave-dwelling vegetarian torn apart by hunting dogs.) This accords with the way he is presented by the comic playwright Aristophanes. In Aristophanes' play *Clouds*, Aeschylus and Euripides are used to embody stuffy traditionalism and new-fangled immorality respectively, with no mention at all of Sophocles (*Clouds* 1364-72). Likewise in Aristophanes' *Frogs*, Aeschylus and Euripides are polarized and pilloried as exemplars of extreme styles of drama—the old-fashioned and the new-fangled—while Sophocles is said to have been a good-tempered man in life and death (*Frogs* 82). We may also note that his style is much harder to parody than that of either of the other two dramatists. All this suggests that Sophocles was elided from the competition of the *Frogs* in part because of his apparently 'moderate' qualities, both personal and poetical. The fact that his year of birth falls between the other two poets has further encouraged this Aristophanic picture of him as a kind of 'mean' between the other two tragedians.

From earliest times, then, Sophocles has been constructed as the most 'serene' and 'ideal' of the dramatists, the one who aimed at and achieved alleged classical canons of moderation and harmony. This idealization of Sophocles as the quintessential classical Greek tragedian has continued to the present day, encouraged by, among other things, the German philosopher Hegel's influential interpretation of *Antigone*. In some ways, this idolatry has benefited the study of Sophocles. But in other ways it has damaged it, by casting an aura of sanctity or dusty respectability over his works, enshrining them as 'classical' and therefore unexciting or impervious to criticism. *King Oidipous*, in particular, has occupied an extraordinary place in the "canon" of the European literary and cultural tradition, and in the modern imagination, thanks in large part to two men: Aristotle and Freud. The former's use of Sophocles' play in the *Poetics*—his treatise on tragedy, whose influence it would be impossible to overstate—made this drama exemplary, enshrined it as the pinnacle of classical Greek tragic art. As for Freud, his thinking has so permeated contemporary culture that the name of Oidipous is, for many readers, more strongly associated with him than with

Sophocles.[3] Indeed, one of our more challenging tasks as readers of Sophocles' play is to remember that at the time it was written, Freud had not yet been born. Nonetheless, we must do our best to approach *King Oidipous*, like all Sophocles' plays, with an open mind, paying close attention to the text itself and its cultural context, and remaining alert to the biases introduced, whether consciously or otherwise, by our own cultural accretions.

THEATER AND PERFORMANCE[4]

The form of drama that we call 'Greek' tragedy was in fact a peculiarly Athenian art form, closely associated with the life of Athens in the fifth century BCE. The theater was enormously popular, in a way which may be hard to grasp today since there is no direct modern equivalent. Athenian dramatic performances combined the official status of a public institution (both civic and religious), the broad popularity of a major Hollywood production, the emotional and competitive appeal of a major sporting event, and the artistic and cultural pre-eminence of Shakespeare. The theater was so far from being an elitist form of entertainment that a fund was instituted to enable poor citizens to buy tickets. Audiences were as large as 15,000-20,000, out of a population of only about 300,000 men, women and children (including slaves and resident aliens).

The exact composition of the audience is, however, a matter of controversy. In particular, scholars are not entirely agreed on whether women were permitted to attend. The traditional assumption that they could not is based on the general exclusion of women from most public arenas of Athenian life. But the main exceptions to this exclusion were religious. Women were able, and indeed required, to go out in public for such events as religious festivals and funerals. And drama at Athens was produced only at public festivals of this kind, held in honor of Dionysos, god of the theater. Moreover Dionysos was a god whose myths embraced all kinds of outsiders. Women played an important part in his cult, in contrast to that of most other major male divinities. This reinforces the slight concrete evidence we have, which suggests that women, along with

---

3 For a brief introductory account of Freud's use of Sophocles' play see Segal 2001: 39-42.

4 An expanded version of this section appears in the introduction to *Women on the Edge: Four Plays by Euripides*, translated with introductions and commentary by Ruby Blondell, Mary-Kay Gamel, Nancy Sorkin Rabinowitz and Bella Zweig (Routledge: New York 1999). For a full discussion, with ancient sources translated into English, see Csapo and Slater 1995.

other socially marginal groups, including even slaves, were indeed permitted to attend the theater. It seems likely, however, that these socially inferior groups would have been present in much smaller numbers than the male citizens who were the dramatists' primary audience.

Dionysos is associated with song and dance, masking and shifting identities, wine and irrational frenzy, vegetation, sex, fertility and growth. He is thus an apt patron for an art form that celebrates the crossing of boundaries and the playing of roles. It was at his principal Athenian festival, the City Dionysia, that most of the great tragedians' works were first performed. At the beginning of this festival a statue of the god was carried in a torchlight procession to the theater, and it remained present throughout the dramas. But the plays were not religious rituals in any modern sense. Drama may have arisen from ritual, and often makes use of ritual forms such as sacrifice, wedding and funeral rites. But drama was not *itself* a ritual. Playwrights and performers were, of course, honoring the gods by their work, but there is no suggestion in our sources that the results were evaluated using religious criteria.

The festival of Dionysos, which lasted several days, included processions, sacrifices, and musical and dramatic performances of various kinds. It was a major civic as well as religious celebration, an occasion for public festivity and civic pride, and an opportunity for Athens to display itself and its cultural achievements to the world. The City Dionysia took place in the spring, when the sailing season had begun and visitors from all over the Greek world might be in town, including the members of the Delian League, who brought their tribute to Athens at this time of year. This tribute was displayed in the theater during the festival. Other related ceremonies included the awarding of golden crowns to public benefactors and the presentation of sets of armor to young men whose fathers had been killed in battle. All this offers striking testimony to the political context in which Athenian drama was originally performed. We should bear this in mind when seeking to understand a play such as *King Oidipous*, whose central themes include the relationship of the individual to society at large and the proper conduct of a ruler. The primary subject matter of tragedy is traditional mythology, but this material is used to scrutinize the political and cultural ideology of the poets' own time, including democracy, gender norms, and Athenian identity.

The tragedies at the City Dionysia were produced as part of a competition. Greek culture generally was highly competitive, and religious festivals often involved various kinds of contest.

The Olympic games are one prominent example, and the City Dionysia itself included contests in comedy and choral song as well as tragedy. The tragic competition lasted for three days, with each poet producing three tragedies followed by one satyr play in the course of a single day. The five judges who decided the contest were carefully selected by an elaborate procedure designed to prevent undue influence and bribes, and their decision was made under pressure from a highly rambunctious crowd. The winning playwright and *chorēgos* or chorus-director (see below) were publicly announced, crowned with ivy (a plant sacred to Dionysos), and had their names inscribed on a marble monument. Sophocles was extremely successful, winning at least eighteen victories and never coming third in the competition.

Sometimes the three tragedies offered by a single playwright would constitute a connected trilogy, like Aeschylus' *Oresteia*, and even the satyr play might be on a related theme. But Sophocles seems to have preferred individual, self-contained dramas. Like the *Oresteia*, his three 'Theban' plays—*Antigone, King Oidipous*, and *Oidipous at Colonus*—focus on the doings and sufferings of a single royal family over more than one generation. Unlike the *Oresteia*, however, they are not a trilogy. The three plays of the *Oresteia* (the only trilogy that survives) were composed to be produced together in a single performance, following in sequence the fortunes of the house of Atreus. But Sophocles' three plays were written at wide intervals, without following the legendary order of events, and in some respects are inconsistent with each other. Each is a dramatic unity, and they were never intended to be performed together. *King Oidipous* is the earliest of these plays in the mythological sequence of events, but was probably the second to be produced (above, p. 4). Yet allusions in this play and in *Oidipous at Colonus* show that Sophocles had not forgotten the thematic threads connecting his three Theban dramas, and perhaps hoped his audience had not either.

Since only three playwrights were allowed to put on their plays at each festival, even having one's plays produced was a competitive challenge. In keeping with the public nature of the event, a city official was in charge of 'granting a chorus' to three finalists out of those who applied (how he reached his decision is unknown). A wealthy citizen (the *chorēgos*) was appointed to bear most of the production costs, as a kind of prestigious extra taxation. Chief among these costs was the considerable expense of training and costuming the chorus. The poet was his own producer, and originally acted as well, or employed professional actors (Sophocles is said to have been the first to stop acting in his own plays). But around the middle of the fifth century the state also assumed control of allocating a principal actor to each production, and began awarding a prize for the best actor.

The plays were performed in the open-air theater of Dionysos on the south-eastern slope of the Acropolis, where an impressive view of the mountains and coastline of southern Attica stretched beyond the playing area. Performances began at dawn and lasted all day. The action of some plays, such as *Antigone*, begins at dawn, which may be an allusion to daybreak in the actual theater. Once the sun had risen, the size and openness of the theater were enhanced by the bright daylight enveloping performers and audience alike. This generated a very different and specifically more public atmosphere than the darkened theaters and artificial lighting of today. The

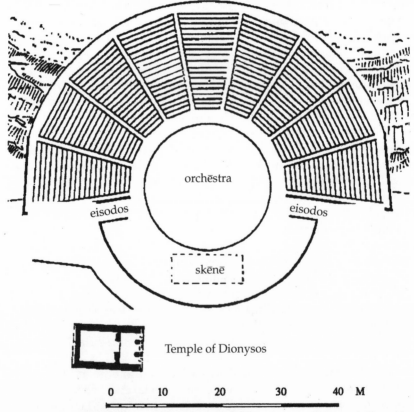

A reconstruction of the theater of Dionysus in Athens during the second half of the fifth century BC. (Based on the sketch by J. Travlos, *Pictorial Dictionary of Ancient Athens* [London 1971] 540.)

audience must have been very conscious of one other as well as of the play, and thus aware of their collective engagement in a public civic and cultural event. They sat crowded together, expressed their opinions, sometimes vociferously, and ate and drank during the performances, especially if they did not approve of the acting. They responded to the plays with visceral emotion, judging them not as aesthetic artefacts remote from real life, but as contributions to the discussion of contemporary political, moral and social concerns. The theater was an extension of their world, not an escape from it.

In size and shape the theater of Dionysos resembled one end of a large football stadium (see diagram, p. 10). The judges sat in carved stone seats at the front, along with the priests of Dionysos and other religious figures, public benefactors, high-ranking officials and important foreign vistors. Most of the audience probably sat on the ground, on the sloping sides of the Acropolis hill above the theater. Foreigners, women, children and slaves were probably seated at the back and sides of the theater. The performance area was dominated by a large dancing floor, the *orchēstra*, which was about seventy feet across. Contemporary scholars are divided over the shape of the *orchēstra* in Sophocles' time. (It may have been round or rectangular.) Behind it was a wooden stage-building, the *skēnē* (literally 'tent' or 'hut') which served as a set. Whether or not there was a raised stage in the fifth century is also a matter of controversy. If so, it was merely a low, narrow platform in front of the stage-building.[5] The *skēnē* had one or more doors through which characters could enter and exit, and was also used by the actors as a changing-room. It usually represents a palace or other structure (as in *King Oidipous* and *Antigone*), but may also serve, for example, as a cave (as in Sophocles' *Philoktetes*), or a grove (*Oidipous at Colonus*). We do not know to what extent such locations were indicated through scene painting and props, but any such indicators were probably stylized and minimal. The theater was so large that detailed scenery would not have been easily visible to the audience.

The main action always takes place outside the stage-building, though interior scenes and scenes from distant locations are often described by the players. Occasionally an interior scene is revealed through the *skēnē* door, usually at a climactic moment (as when Eurydike's corpse is revealed at *Antigone* 1293). Sometimes this was accomplished in performance by means of a device called the

---

[5] For convenience, it is usual in discussing Greek drama to use the word "stage" to refer to the entire performance area, and I have followed that practice.

ekkyklēma, a low wheeled platform that could be rolled out of the *skēnē* to display a tableau from within. This device may have been used at the end of *Antigone*. Entrances and exits not involving the *skēnē*, including the entry and departure of the chorus, were made along the side-entrances—two long ramps, one on each side of the *orchēstra*, called *eisodoi* (or sometimes *parodoi*). The same *eisodos* is used consistently throughout the play to represent a particular locale. In *King Oidipous*, one of them leads to the countryside (and thence to Corinth and Delphi), the other to the city of Thebes proper. The dominant presence of the *skēnē* at the center, and the length of the side-entrances, could both be exploited for dramatic purposes, as when Kreon makes his hesitant first entrance (78-86), or Oidipous emerges blinded from the palace (1298).

The entire 'production team' of Athenian tragedy (playwrights, producers, dancers, musicians, chorus and actors) was male. This extends to the numerous female roles, all of which were played by adult men (not boys, as in Shakespearean drama). The sex, age and status of each character were indicated in a formal, stylized way by costumes and masks. The masks were bold in design, as they had to be if they were to be visible to spectators seated at the far edge of the theater. But they were naturalistic in manner and covered the whole head, including the ears, and had wigs attached. The lavish costumes included long, colorfully decorated robes, and sometimes tall, thin-soled boots. (Grotesque masks and thick-soled 'buskins' came later.) Details of costume and props would make clear the status of each character and might reflect familiar Athenian activities. A king like Oidipous might carry a scepter, and the blind old Teiresias would wear priestly garb and lean on a staff. Such props might be exploited by the playwright to serve dramatically significant functions (cf. Essay p. 103).

The standard number of speaking actors in a given production, apart from the chorus, was three, though there were usually several non-speaking extras playing silent parts such as guards and attendants. The reasons for this restriction to three speaking actors is unknown. But it explains why there are never more than three speaking characters on stage together. It also means that when, as in most plays, there are more than three speaking characters, at least one actor would have to play more than one part. Sometimes, too, a single role had to be split between two or more actors. The latter practice is alien to the standard conventions of modern drama, but it was facilitated by the fact that the actors were all male, and wore not only distinctive costumes but rigid masks which identified each character clearly. Moreover the acting was highly stylized, and did not rely on subtle body movements or facial expressions (which were ruled out by the masks). In such a large theater the actors must have delivered their lines loudly and emphatically, and used broad, clear gestures, in order to be seen and heard.

A central feature of all Athenian tragedies is the chorus, a group of fifteen performers who normally remain present from their entrance until the end of the play. Its members were masked and dressed in character like the main actors. The choral identity is a collective one. In contrast to the heroic individuality of the actors, the chorus are numerous, anonymous, and almost always unanimous. They have no individual names, and they speak and are addressed indiscriminately in the singular or plural. They therefore represent, to a certain extent, the group, as opposed to the individual, showing the effects of the main actors' words and deeds on the larger human community. As a collective group, they are in a sense continuous with the audience whose fellow-citizens they are. But whether we view them as actors or citizens, they form only one segment of the community as a whole. As citizens, they are free adult male Athenians playing a role in the theater. In their dramatic persona, however, they represent, remarkably often, a socially marginal segment of society—women, old men, foreigners, underlings or even slaves. They are thus far from being an embodiment of the Athenian *polis* or of 'society' in the abstract. Even in *King Oidipous*, where they do play the role of elite males, the chorus are old men whose opening song emphasizes their helplessness.

Nor does the chorus represent an 'objective' view of events or the 'voice of the poet." As a character in the drama they have a clearly defined identity, a specific gender and social status, which befit the particular segment of society that they embody, and are important for a proper understanding of the play. Though played by men, their characters are generally of the same sex as the central figure of the drama, with whom they enjoy a certain solidarity. (*Antigone* is unusual in this regard, if we regard Antigone herself as the central character.) The chorus sometimes plays an active role in the story (as in Aeschylus' *Eumenides*), but more usually represents a group of bystanders, whether local citizens or other concerned persons. We do not know how much physical contact took place between chorus and actors, or to what extent they shared the same performance spaces. Sometimes the chorus seem to participate quite vigorously in the stage action (e.g. *Oidipous at Colonus* 829-43). But their dramatic effectiveness is usually quite limited. And their 'personality' is both more bland and more fluid than that of the main characters, as they react to unfolding events.

The primary dramatic medium of the chorus is lyric song and dance, performed in the *orchēstra*, or 'dancing area.' At intervals throughout the drama they perform a choral song, singing and dancing in unison. Although we know little about the choreography, it certainly included a strong mimetic element and drew on the rich living tradition of public choral dance, which was an integral part of many ritual, competitive and festal occasions in Greek life. The accompanying music was simple and did not interfere with comprehension of the words, which are always significant for the drama and sometimes of the highest poetic complexity. Their profundity may at times seem inappropriate to the chorus when viewed in character, e.g. as a group of sailors or slave women. But choral lyrics give the poet a different dramatic idiom in which to explore the themes of the play, and should not be tied too closely to the specific character of the chorus that gives them utterance. Though the sentiments are those of the choral character, the richness and complexity with which they are expressed often open up wider horizons and more diverse points of view than this particular social group could be aware of.

Greek tragedy is structured around the alternation of speech and song. Most plays open with a spoken monologue or dialogue by the actors (the prologue), which sets the scene and provides the audience with any necessary background information. Sophocles characteristically accomplishes this exposition through conversation, which simultaneously introduces important characters. This opening scene is followed by the arrival of the chorus, who enter singing the *parodos* or 'entry song.' They normally remain in the *orchēstra* for the rest of the play, performing further songs with dancing (known as *stasima* or 'songs in position') between the scenes of the drama, and participating to some extent in the action. This alternation of actors' speech and choral song is a fluid form rather than a rigid structure. Actors will sometimes shift into lyric meters, or converse with the chorus in a sung dialogue, especially at moments of high emotion (such as the emergence of the blinded Oidipous from the palace). Such a dialogue may play the scene-dividing role of a choral ode, or serve to vary the tone of a long scene. Conversely the chorus had a leader (the *koruphaios*), who not only led the dancing but exchanged a few spoken lines with the actors, serving as the mouthpiece of the chorus as a whole. Since it is not always clear exactly when the *koruphaios* is speaking for the chorus, in most translations, including this one, all choral passages are attributed simply to the chorus.

Both the spoken and the sung portions of Athenian drama are composed in verse. Greek poetry is not structured through rhyme, but depends on rhythmic patterns (meters) to create poetic form. The lyric songs are composed in highly varied and elaborate meters, unique to each song. A typical choral ode consists of a series of pairs of stanzas called the 'strophe' and 'antistrophe.' Each strophe has its own complex rhythmic structure, which is repeated precisely in the antistrophe. There may be several such strophic pairs, each metrically unique. Occasionally the strophe and antistrophe will echo each other linguistically or structurally as well as metrically (compare e.g. lines 168 and 178, 872 and 882, 895-6 and 909-10). The strophic pair may be followed by an epode—an additional single stanza with its own unique metrical pattern (as at *Antigone* 876-82). Though the spoken portions of Greek drama may be highly emotional—for example in the rhetorical expression of anger—lyrics are most often the vehicle for intense emotions such as grief or pity, which they express in a more impressionistic, less rational style than spoken dialogue.

The actors' spoken lines, by contrast, are in iambic trimeters, a regular six-beat meter approximating the flow of natural speech (rather like Shakespearean blank verse). Other meters are occasionally used, especially anapests, a regular 'marching' rhythm often associated with entrances and exits. Anapests were probably chanted rather than spoken or sung. (They are printed in italics in the translation.) The actors' spoken speeches range in length from the long rhetorical oration, or *rhēsis*, to stichomythia, a formal kind of dialogue in which the characters exchange single alternating lines, or occasionally two lines apiece. King Oidipous has many long stretches of stichomythia, a mode well suited to the gradual disclosure of information that is so central to the play. Such modes of speech, like many other aspects of Greek tragedy, may strike the modern audience as artificial. But every kind of drama relies on its own formal conventions. We tend not to notice the artificiality of our own theater (including film), because familiarity makes its conventions seem natural to us.

Mythic background

The principal subject matter of Athenian tragedy is traditional Greek mythology. But there was no official canon of such tales, and no requirement that various versions should be consistent. The dramatists and their audiences were exposed to many versions of the myths, oral and written, traditional and innovative, in varying contexts which affected their mode of presentation and their meanings (epic recitation, theatrical performance, religious ritual, oral tale-telling, and so on). The tragedians and other writers were also free to create their own innovations in the stories. Some central features of the myths may have been in practice unchangeable (the Greeks always win the Trojan war), but the degree of possible variation that remains may surprise the modern reader (Helen does not necessarily go to Troy; Medea does not always kill her children). A dramatist was also free to vary the character traits even of well-known figures, for example by making a traditional personality more or less sympathetic. Mythology was therefore a highly flexible medium for the ancient dramatists, enabling them to draw on past traditions and present expectations while adding their own developments to the future store of tales. But our own knowledge of these rich and varied traditions is scanty. It remains helpful for our understanding of the plays to reconstruct as best we can any versions that we know to have been current in the poet's own day. Yet we must bear in mind that countless stories unknown to us undoubtedly influenced the dramatists' practice and helped to shape the plays' meanings for their original audience.

Oidipous was the most famous mythic king of Thebes, a very ancient city some thirty miles northwest of Athens (see Maps 1 and 2). His family history formed the subject of several lost epic poems and was an extremely popular subject in poetry and art, both before and during Sophocles' lifetime. Sophocles himself composed three surviving dramas about this family and the terrible events that befell it: *Antigone*, *Oidipous the King*, and *Oidipous at Colonus*. These plays exemplify the tendency of Athenian tragedy to locate disturbing mythological events beyond the territory of Athens itself. Thebes, in particular—a historical enemy of Athens—serves as a kind of ideological alter ego or 'anti-Athens,' used to embody and explore cultural tensions that might be highly disturbing to the audience if dramatized in an Athenian setting.[6] Athens and Athenians, by contrast, usually behave impeccably in Athenian drama. In *Oidipous at Colonus*, for example, Athens under its idealized king Theseus serves as the enlightened and generous haven of refuge for Oidipous, after he has been exiled by the Thebans.

Oidipous is most familiar to the modern mind as Sophocles' famous hero, who falls from the pinnacle of human accomplishment

---

6   On this issue see F. Zeitlin, "Thebes: Theater of Self and Society in Athenian Drama," in Winkler and Zeitlin 1990: 130-67 and M. W. Blundell, 'The Ideal of the *Polis* in *Oedipus at Colonus*,' in *Tragedy, Comedy and the Polis*, ed. A.H. Sommerstein, S. Halliwell, J. Henderson and B. Zimmermann (Bari, Italy 1993) p. 287-306. The only surviving drama in which an Athenian king behaves dubiously is Euripides' *Hippolytos*, which is not set in Athens itself, but in Troezen (see Map 2).

to the depths of an excruciating self-awareness, blinding himself when he discovers that he has unwittingly killed his father, Laios, and married his own mother, Jokasta. He has become a universal symbol not only of the tragic blindness of the human condition, but also, thanks to the incalculable influence of Freud, of the deepest and most terrible fears and desires of the unconscious. The earliest myth of Oidipous, however, makes him no such figure of doom, despite the parricide and incest that are part of his story from the beginning. There was an epic on the subject that is now lost, but the very little we know of it suggests that it diverged considerably from the accounts in tragedy. In the *Odyssey* we hear that though Oidipous was distressed at the discovery of his deeds, he went on ruling at Thebes (11.271-80). There is no mention of oracles or of Oidipous' self-blinding, though his mother/wife does hang herself. The *Iliad* mentions that he died violently—perhaps in battle or a fight—and was honored at Thebes with funeral games (23.679-80). Other treatments prior to that of Sophocles included a tragedy by Aeschylus. Though this too is lost, we know that it included the Sphinx and Oidipous' self-blinding, and probably focused more on the family curse than does Sophocles' play.

King Oidipous opens upon Oidipous as the King of Thebes, beloved by his people, an intelligent, confident and compassionate man in the prime of life. We learn in the course of the play that he was raised in Corinth, but left that city to consult Apollo's oracle at Delphi about his parentage. Apollo, one of the most important gods of the Greek pantheon, is the patron of many areas of human life, including prophecy, archery, music and poetry, sickness and healing, light, purification and self-understanding. His principle oracle, at Delphi, retained considerable political as well as religious importance throughout the classical period. This oracle gives Oidipous the horrible prediction that he will kill his father and marry his mother. His reaction is to leave his parents at Corinth behind in order to prevent the prophecy from coming true. This illustrates the important fact that although prophecies and oracles were pervasive and extremely important, Greeks typically did not view these messages from the gods as deterministic predictions that impaired their own freedom of action. Though a typically pious Greek would expect such prophecies to come true in some sense (as long as they were derived from a legitimate source), such fulfilment might take unexpected forms. Thus Jokasta, in this play, points out to Oidipous that people often perform transgressive actions in dreams (980-82), which might count as the fulfilment of a prophecy (see further Essay, pp. 106-7).

Oidipous travels away from his "parents" in Corinth in the direction of Thebes. On his way, he is provoked by an unknown man at a fork in the road, and kills him. Proceeding on to Thebes, he finds the city terrorized by the Sphinx, a winged monster with a lion's body and a woman's head and breasts. The Sphinx had entered Greek mythology from Egyptian tradition by the Bronze Age, and is a popular theme in Greek art, especially on tombstones. She is first mentioned in literature by Hesiod (*Theog.* 326-32). Unlike the Egyptian Sphinx (but like some near-eastern equivalents), she is both female and winged. Like many other such figures in mythology (Sirens, Gorgons, Furies, Keres etc.), she is a bringer of death, who binds and entraps men. She is often eroticized, preying on youths on the verge of manhood, whom she carries off and kills. In the Oidipous myth, she kills anyone who cannot answer a riddle. Her name may mean "strangler," and the riddle is an intellectual form of weaving or entrapment (cf. 130, 391).

One version of the Sphinx's famous riddle, which may go back to a lost tragedy, runs: "Two-footed and four-footed and three-footed upon the earth, it has a single voice, and alone of all those on land or in the air or sea it changes form. And when it goes supported on three feet, then the speed of its limbs is weakest."[7] The answer is "a human being," who in the course of a life-time (often likened in Greek imagery to the passage of a day) goes first on four feet (a crawling baby), then on two (an adult) and finally on three (two legs and a walking stick). Like the enigmatic Sphinx herself, who is made up of human, bird and beast, the human creature's identity is made up of a complex fusion of roles whose meaning must be deciphered. With her riddling speech delivered in hexameter verse, the Sphinx is also a kind of malevolent counterpart to Apollo, god of prophecy, whose oracles—likewise delivered in hexameters—were typically riddling in their language and easily misunderstood. On his temple at Delphi was inscribed the injunction "know yourself."

Oidipous solves the riddle, thus causing the Sphinx's death and saving the city from her depradations. In gratitude, the Thebans give him the crown of their recently murdered king, Laios, and the hand of the queen in marriage. This pattern of events is familiar from many myths and folktales. But Oidipous' story inverts the usual happy ending. In the course of Sophocles' drama he discovers that he is actually the son of Laios, who was the unknown man at the crossroads, and Jokasta, who is now his own wife. Oidipous has inherited his malignant doom from his father Laios, who (at least

---

7 This translation is taken from Gantz (1993) 496.

according to some versions of the myth) offended the gods and was warned by Apollo not to have any children. This is mentioned, for example, by Aeschylus (*Seven Against Thebes* 742-52). When *Oidipous at Colonus* alludes to the doom or curse that lies over the house of Oidipous (e.g. 369, 596, 965), this may be traced back not only to Oidipous' own deeds, but to those of his father before him. So too in *Antigone*, the doom on the house of Oidipous is clearly marked at the outset (1-6), and persists as a background theme of the play (49-60, 593-603, 856-71). But in *King Oidipous* this aspect of the story receives little emphasis. The family curse is only touched on, and no blame is ascribed to Laios, since the oracle he receives is simply a prediction, not an injunction.

When Oidipous discovers the dreadful truth about himself, he puts out his eyes in horror and longs only to go into exile from Thebes. Since he acted in ignorance and (in the case of the parricide) in self-defence, he would be found innocent in a court of law, ancient as well as modern. But legal guilt and innocence have little to do with the kind of horror aroused by such revelations. Despite his innocence, Oidipous is a polluted man—a tainted outcast who risks bringing divine retribution not only on himself, but on all who associate with him. Religious pollution, or miasma, is caused by various kinds of crimes and transgressions, especially murder, whether it is intentional or not. It is not the same as guilt, since a legally and morally innocent person may still be polluted, for example by causing an accidental death. In Athenian law, such persons could normally free themselves from pollution by carrying out certain rituals of purification. But Oidipous' pollution is uniquely terrible and infectious, owing to the appallingly transgressive nature of his inadvertent deeds, which no simple ritual can cleanse. The only way to free Thebes from the contamination of his presence is leave the city and go into exile, which might also provide a measure of purification for himself by distancing him, in space and time, from his polluting deeds. But at the end of *King Oidipous* his fate is left uncertain, since Kreon, his brother-in-law, uncle, and successor as king, will not allow him to go into exile without first—once again—consulting Apollo's oracle at Delphi (see further Essay, p. 131-2).

Some twenty years later Sophocles, by now an old man himself, returned to complete the story of Oidipous in his last play, *Oidipous at Colonus*. Throughout this long drama the events of *King Oedipus* are recalled, especially in Oidipous' reiterated self-defense for the terrible deeds of his past (*OC* 265-74, 521-48, 960-1002). The later tragedy also dramatically reverses Oidipous' fall from greatness in the earlier one. This time he starts out at the nadir of his fortunes and grows into a figure of heroic stature. At the start of the play he has been wandering in exile from Thebes for many years, with only Antigone as his guide, companion and protector. At the end, he proceeds to an awe-inspiring and uniquely miraculous death, which establishes him as an Athenian cult hero, to be honored and placated for the protection of the city. It was in this capacity that he would have been most familiar to Sophocles' original audience: awe-inspiring not only as a paradigm of human misery, but as a heroic figure exerting supernatural power from beyond the grave.

KING OIDIPOUS

CHARACTERS
OIDIPOUS, king of Thebes
PRIEST of Zeus
KREON, brother of Jokasta
CHORUS of aged Theban noblemen
TEIRESIAS, a prophet
JOKASTA, wife of Oidipous
FIRST MESSENGER (a poor old man from Corinth)
SHEPHERD (an aged slave of the royal house)
SECOND MESSENGER (a servant from within the house)
Antigone and Ismene, daughters of Oidipous and Jokasta
Guards and attendants

[Setting: Outside the palace of Oidipous and Jokasta at Thebes. The scene shows the façade of the house, which has a central door. Near the door is an altar of the god Apollo. One of the two side-entrances represents the road to the countryside (and thence to Corinth and Delphi), the other the way to the city of Thebes proper.]

[Oidipous enters from the palace, a man in the prime of life whose costume indicates royal status and authority. Before him is a crowd of citizens of all ages, carrying olive or laurel branches twined with wool and sitting on the steps of the altar. In front of them stands the priest of Zeus.[1] Oidipous addresses the crowd in iambic trimeters, the meter of dialogue (above, p. 14).]

OIDIPOUS
My children, youngest nurslings of your ancestor
Kadmos,[2] why do you sit here so beseechingly,

---

1 Zeus is the chief god and patriarchal king of the ancient Greek pantheon. He is the ruler of the Olympian gods and oversees many aspects of human life, including kingship, hospitality, supplication, justice, oaths and friendship.
2 Kadmos was the founder of Thebes and Laios' great-grandfather. This, of course, makes him Oidipous' own ancestor as well, but at this point in the play he is unaware of that fact.

bearing these suppliant branches garlanded with wool?[3]
The city is filled up alike with incense-smoke,
alike with prayers to Paian and with groaning cries.[4]   5
I thought it was not right for me to hear this by
report from others, children, so I've come myself:
I, famed to everyone, the man called Oidipous.

[He turns to the priest of Zeus.]

Come, tell me, aged one—since you're the natural
and fitting spokesman for these others—why you're sitting   10
here: in dread or in desire? You can be sure
I wish to aid you fully. I would be immune
to grief, did I not pity suppliants like these.

PRIEST

Oh Oidipous! Oh you who rule my land in power!
You see what age we are who sit here at your altar—   15
some who are still not strong enough to flutter far,
others already burdened with the weight of age;
I am the priest of Zeus, and these are chosen youths;
the other Thebans, branches wreathed with wool, are sitting
in the market-places and at both the shrines   20
of Pallas and Ismenos's prophetic ash.[5]
As you yourself can see, the city's now so badly
storm-tossed that it can no longer keep its head
from sinking down below the tossing waves of blood;
it is decaying in the fruitful husks of earth,   25

---

3 Supplication was a ritual whereby people in trouble sought help by
   sitting at a more powerful person's feet or at an altar. It involved various
   ritual gestures, especially touching the cheek or knees of the person
   supplicated, and sometimes props such as the branches wreathed with
   wool referred to here. Suppliants were under the protection of Zeus as
   well as the god at whose altar they sat (if any). Supplication exerted
   moral and religious pressure on the more powerful person to grant
   the suppliant's request.
4 Paian is a healing god closely associated with Apollo (Introduction, p. 17),
   with whom he is sometimes identified (see below, line 155 with note).
5 Thebes had at least two market-places. Pallas is a common name for
   the goddess Athena, who had two temples in Thebes. Ismenos was one
   of the main rivers of Thebes, often used to identify the city. "Prophetic
   ash" probably refers to a temple of Apollo, god of prophecy, which
   stood near the river, and where divination was practised by means of
   burned sacrificial victims (cf. below, n. on 311).

decaying in the herds of pastured cattle and
in women's barren labor-pains; the fiery god
has swooped down, a most hateful plague, to scourge
the city, emptying the house of Kadmos while
black Hades is enriched with groaning and laments.[6]   30
It's not because we judge you equal to the gods
that I and these, your children, sit here at your hearth,[7]
but as the first of men, both in life's circumstances
and in dealings with divinities.[8] For you
came to the town of Kadmos and released it from   35
the tribute we were paying the harsh singer,[9] though
you had no special knowledge and had not been taught
by us; no, it was through the aid of god that you
set our lives straight again—so people think and say.[10]

  Now, royal Oidipous, most powerful to all,   40
we do beseech you, all those here as suppliants,
to find us some protection, whether you have heard
a god's voice, or perhaps know something from a man;[11]

---

6   The god Hades is the lord of the underworld and king over the dead.
    There is a rich interweaving of imagery in this description of the blight
    on the land, which takes three forms: sterility of crops, sterility or
    still-birth of humans, and the plague itself, which is likened both to a
    military enemy and to fire (associated with disease through fever). The
    ancient image of the ship of state, which recurs repeatedly throughout
    the play, is here linked with the image of the state as an individual
    drowning in a sea of blood.
7   A domestic altar and a hearth were to some degree interchangeable. The
    hearth, which normally lay in a house's courtyard, was the symbolic as
    well as the literal center of the household, and as such was sacred both
    to Hestia, goddess of the hearth, and to Zeus.
8   The word translated as "circumstances" is ominous, since it is usually
    used for disasters (cf. 833, 1347, 1525).
9   The Sphinx demanded "tribute" in the form of the lives of those
    who failed to answer her riddle. She is called a 'singer' because she
    chanted her riddles in hexameter verse, the same meter used by epic
    poetry and the Delphic oracle. At line 391 she is called a 'song-weaver'
    (*rhapsidos*)—the same word used for professional reciters of epic. See
    further Introduction, p. 18.
10 Language of setting straight or upright (the same word in Greek) recurs
    throughout the play (39; cf. 50, 88, 419, 506, 528, 696, 853, 1222).
11 The line ends with the words *oistha pou*, meaning 'perhaps you know.'
    This is the first of many untranslatable puns on the name of Oidipous
    (see further Essay, pp. 98-9).

for it is those with past experience, I've seen,
whose plans most often stay alive through their success.   45
Come, best of mortals, make our city stand up straight!
Come, think about yourself as well: this land now calls
you savior for your heartfelt vigor in the past;
may this, your rule, not be remembered as the time
when after standing straight we fell back down again.   50
No, stand this city upright in security!
Back then you offered us good fortune blessed by a
well-omened bird:[12] be equal to that now as well.
If you're to rule this land in power, as you do now,
it's finer to hold power with living men than in   55
a desert; walls are nothing, nor are ships, if they
are emptied of the men who dwelt in them with you.

OIDIPOUS

Pitiful children, known—and not unknown—to me
are the desires that bring you here; for I know well
that all of you are sick; and yet, sick as you are,   60
there is not one of you whose sickness equals mine.
Your grief afflicts each person individually,
in isolation from the rest; *my* spirit, though,
groans for the city, and myself, and you as well.
You are not waking someone who was fast asleep;   65
know that I have already let fall many tears
and travelled many wandering roads of anxious thought.
And looking closely into it I only found
one cure, which I've enacted: I have sent Kreon,
Menoikeus' son, my own wife's brother, to Apollo's   70
Pythian home,[13] inquiring how I may succeed
in rescuing this city through my deeds or words.
And as I measure up the days, the passing time
pains me. How is he faring? He has now been gone
unreasonably long, beyond the fitting time.   75
But when he does arrive, I would be evil if
I did not act on everything the god reveals.

12 The "bird of good omen" is metaphorical, but alludes to the practice of
    divniation by observing birds (see below, n. on 311)
13 Apollo is the principal god of prophecy, and "Pythian" is one of his most
    common epithets. His "Pythian home" is Delphi, his most important
    oracle, also called Pytho (e.g. below, 153).

PRIEST
> Your words are opportune; these people here just gave
> a sign to me that Kreon is approaching us.

*[Enter Kreon along the side-entrance leading from Delphi, wearing a wreath
of bay laurel—a plant sacred to Apollo—as a sign of success.]*

OIDIPOUS
> Oh lord Apollo, may he come to us with bright   80
> and saving fortune, even as his eyes are bright!

PRIEST
> His news is sweet, so I surmise; or else he would
> not come towards us crowned with thickly berried bay.

OIDIPOUS
> We'll soon know, now he measures close enough to hear.
> My lord, Menoikeus' son and my own kin, what message   85
> has your arrival brought us from the voice of god?

KREON
> A good one! Even what is hard to bear, I say,
> may end up in good fortune, if it comes out straight.

OIDIPOUS
> What were his actual words? What you have said so far
> fills me with neither confidence nor apprehension.   90

KREON
> If you desire to hear me talk with these folk present
> I'm prepared to do so—or to go inside.

OIDIPOUS
> Speak out before us all! I bear a greater weight
> of sorrow for these people than for my own life.

KREON
> I'll say, then, what I heard the god divulge. My lord,   95
> Phoibos commands us clearly to drive out a taint
> upon this land that has been nurtured here, and not
> to nurse this thing until it is incurable.[14]

OIDIPOUS
> To cleanse ourselves? But how? And from what circumstance?

---

14 Phoibos ("Bright") is a common name for Apollo, who is associated
    with light and sometimes identified with Helios, god of the sun.
    On religious taint, or pollution—a notion central to this play—see
    Introduction, p. 19.

KREON

By driving someone out, or paying blood for blood,   100
since blood is what engulfs our city in this storm.

OIDIPOUS

Does he declare upon what man this fortune fell?

KREON

My lord, before you steered our city's course aright,
a man called Laios was the ruler of this land.

OIDIPOUS

I know of him—though just from hearsay, not by sight.   105

KREON

He's dead; and now the god commands us clearly to
lay hands in vengeance on the men who murdered him.

OIDIPOUS

And where on earth are they? Where will the doubtful track
of evidence be found for such an ancient crime?

KREON

Here in this land, he said. If something is sought out   110
it can be captured, while what is ignored escapes.

OIDIPOUS

Did this man Laios fall in with his bloody death
at home, or in the fields, or in some other land?

KREON

He left here to consult the oracle, he said,
but after setting out he never came back home.[15]   115

OIDIPOUS

And was there no report, no fellow-traveler
who saw something of use, from whom one might have learned?

KREON

All died but one, who fled in fear, and he could tell
with knowledge nothing that he saw—except one thing.

OIDIPOUS

And what was that? One fact might lead to learning much,   120
if we could grasp some small beginning-point of hope.

---

15 Sophocles does not say why Laios was consulting the Delphic oracle,
    but in other versions of the story he was going to inquire whether
    the baby he and his wife exposed on the mountain to die had in fact
    perished (cf. Introduction, pp. 18-19).

KREON

He said the robbers that they met killed Laios not
with one man's strength, but by the blows of many hands.

OIDIPOUS

How could the robber dare to go so far, unless
he was suborned with silver from some Theban source?   125

KREON

That was our thinking; but with Laios dead, no one
arose as our defender at an evil time.

OIDIPOUS

What evil underfoot, the kingdom having fallen
thus, kept you from learning fully what transpired?

KREON

The devious-singing Sphinx led us to set aside   130
the mystery and look at what lay at our feet.[16]

OIDIPOUS

I'll start again then, and reveal these things as well.
For fittingly has Phoibos, and you fittingly,
paid such attention on behalf of him who died.
So you will see me also as their ally justly   135
taking vengeance for this land and for the god.
I shall disperse this taint, not on behalf of some
more distant friend or kinsman, but for my own self,
since he—whoever killed that man—may wish perhaps
to use the same avenging hand against me too.   140
By aiding Laios, then, I also help myself.[17]

    Come now, my children, stand up from the steps as fast
as possible; remove these suppliant branches, and
let someone gather Kadmos' people here; be sure
that I'll do everything I can. We shall, with god's

16   Lines 128-31 provide the first, apparently innocuous, appearances of
the "foot" motif, which links Oidipous' name both with the riddle of
the Sphinx and with the pervasive theme of physical and intellectual
travel (Essay, p. 98).

17   The preceding lines are heavily ironic, since Oidipous is himself his father's
closest kinsman (137-8). The word "justly" (135) suggests the obligation
he would have, in Athenian law, to investigate the murder of his father
as next of kin. His fear that the killer will turn "the same hand" on him in
vengeance (139-40) will be literally fulfilled, when he puts out his own eyes.
And by aiding Laios he will not help, but destroy himself.

help, be revealed as fortunate or fallen men.   145

[*Exit Oidipous into the palace, and Kreon along the side-entrance leading to the city.*]

PRIEST

My children, let us stand. He's just announced to us
the very favor for the sake of which we came.
May Phoibos, who has sent these oracles, come both
to save us and to bring our sickness to an end.   150

[*Exeunt priest and suppliants along the side-entrance leading to the city. Enter the chorus of Theban noblemen, representing the mass of the people just summoned by Oidipous. They proceed into the orchēstra, singing and dancing the parodos or entry-song.*]

CHORUS

Oh sweet-spoken Voice of Zeus,   *Strophe A*
meaning what have you come
from gold-rich Pytho to gleaming Thebes?[18]
Mind racked with fear, I quiver with dread,
Delian Paian to whom we cry aloud, in awe at you;[19]   155
What debt will you ordain—something new,
or one that returns as the seasons revolve?[20]
Tell me, child of golden hope, immortal Voice!

---

18 Pytho is another name for Delphi, to whose oracular Voice the chorus address their song (for the personification compare 158 and 188). Zeus is viewed as the author of the oracle, both because he is the ultimate ruler of human events and because Apollo is his son, and serves as his messenger. Delphi was famously "rich in gold," both because it served as a kind of bank for the storage of precious metals and because of the numerous lavish offerings dedicated there by worshipers.

19 On Paian see above, n. on 5. Here the god is addressed as Delian because he is identified with Apollo, who was born on the island of Delos. Apollo was a god who brought both plague (as at the beginning of the *Iliad*) and healing (as he is asked to do here). Here the chorus identify the plague itself not with Apollo but with Ares (190). Apollo, as the god most deeply implicated in Oidipous' story, is also obviously in some sense the cause of the plague, but there is no reason for the chorus to suspect this.

20 The contrast is between the possible need to propitiate the gods for some new occurrence, and the revival of Thebes' past troubles with the Sphinx and Laios, which may turn out to be causally connected with the plague, and as such require a reiterated "payment" to the gods.

I call first on you, daughter of Zeus,
    immortal Athena.   *Antistrophe A*
I beseech too your sister Artemis, our land's support,   160
who sits on her glorious circular throne
in the market-place, and far-shooting Apollo.
Appear to me as three-fold protectors from doom,
if you banished the flames of disaster
when doom rushed over our city   165
in the past, come now as well!²¹

Oh, oh! Uncountable   *Strophe B*
are the troubles I endure!
My whole company is sick;²²
there's no spear of thought to protect us;   170
the offspring of the glorious earth grows not,
nor do women emerge with births
from the labor-pains where they cry aloud.²³
You may see one after another
like a strong-winged bird,   175
speeding swifter than savage fire
to the shores of the evening god.²⁴

---

21 The chorus invoke a triad of important gods: Athena (patron goddess of Athens), Apollo, and Artemis, his twin sister (goddess of hunting and animals). Apollo is called "far-shooting" because his primary weapon is the bow. It is a common feature of prayers to invoke past benefits bestowed by the divinity in question.

22 The language suggests a ship's company, thus once again evoking the ship of state.

23 The procreation of children and production of crops are very closely associated in Greek culture, and frequently represented as parallel or identical processes (cf. 25-7, 260; *Ant.* 569). Since these homologous processes are both vital to the flourishing of human life, the anger of the gods is expressed through a parallel blight on both kinds of reproduction, as well as in the plague as such.

24 The 'evening god' is Hades, whose realm is sometimes located in the west, and who is fittingly associated with the darkness of sunset, since this symbolizes the loss of the light of life. In early Greek art, the souls of the dead are often represented as winged creatures. In Homer, they are likened to a fluttering cloud of bats. Here, they are envisaged as a flock of birds streaming westward into a fiery sunset. At the same time, the fire imagery recalls the burning pyres that consume the bodies of the dead.

Through these deaths beyond count   *Antistrophe B*
the city perishes;
offspring lie on the plain unpitied,   180
unmourned, bringing yet more death.[25]
Wives and white-haired women
ring the altars in supplication
lamenting their grievous pains.
The Paian shines forth,[26]   185
and voices groan in accompaniment;
for all these things, oh golden daughter of Zeus,[27]
send us the fair face of Protection!

Grant that raging Ares, who flames at me now,   *Strophe C*
attacking without the bronze of shields,   191
surrounded by screaming,
turn his back on my fatherland
and run rushing in retreat,
wafted away to Amphitrite's great bed-chamber,   195
or the Thracian waves inhospitable to anchorage;[28]
for if night leaves something undone,
the day undertakes to complete it.[29]
Oh you who wield the power
of fire-bearing lightning,   200
oh father Zeus, destroy him
with your thunderbolt!

Lykeian lord,[30] I also wish   *Antistrophe C*

25 This presumably refers to the contagiousness of the rotting corpses.
26 The Paian is a song of thanksgiving to Apollo or another god, or, as in
    this case, a prayer for protection or healing.
27 The chorus is again addressing Athena, to whom they will add Zeus,
    Apollo and finally Dionysos (Bacchus).
28 Amphitrite is wife of the sea-god Poseidon, and her "bed-chamber"
    is the Atlantic Ocean. The "Thracian waves" refer to the Black Sea.
    These two bodies of water represent, to the choral imagination, the
    most remote locations to east and west, to which they hope Ares will
    be dispatched.
29 The exact meaning of these two lines, and their relationship to the
    context, are both uncertain.
30 "Lykeian" is a frequent epithet of Apollo, of uncertain meaning and origin.
    Since it resembles a root meaning "light," it connotes primarily brightness
    (a chief attribute of this god). But it also evokes the epithet Lycian (see n.on

the invincible arrows
from your gold-spun bowstring   205
to spread out, stationed in our defense,
and the gleamings of Artemis' fiery torches,
with which she darts through the Lycian mountains;[31]
and I call on the god of the golden head-dress,
who shares his name with this land,   210
Bakkhos, face flushed with wine,
companion of the Maenads,
whose worshipers cry aloud *Euoi*,
to approach us flaming with gleaming pine-torch
and attack the god dishonored among gods.[32]   215

[As the chorus conclude their song, Oidipous re-enters from the palace.]

OIDIPOUS
You pray: as for these prayers, if you are willing to
listen and take my words in, ministering to
your sickness, you may gain protection and lift up
your heads above these evils. I shall speak as one
who's foreign to this story, foreign to the deed,   220
for I could not get far in tracking it without
some clue. Since I did not become a citizen
till later, I proclaim to all you Kadmeans:
if anyone among you knows the man who killed
Laios, the son of Labdakos, I now command   225
that person to provide me with a full report.
If he's afraid, let him eliminate the charge
                    * * * * * * * * * * *
by coming forward, and he'll suffer nothing worse

208), and sometimes alludes to Apollo's role as a protector—specifically,
against wolves—since the root *lyk-* resembles the word for a wolf (*lykos*).

31   Lycia is a region of Asia Minor, often associated with Apollo, and in this
case with his sister Artemis as well.

32   Ares, god of war, is often said to be unpopular with the other gods.
Dionysos (Bacchus), god of wine and theater, is associated with the east
and sometimes represented as wearing an orientalized head-dress.
He was an important god of Thebes, which was his birthplace. He is
often referred to as "Theban," while Thebes is called "Bacchic." The
Maenads were female worshippers who followed him in his travels
and participated in his festivities (where pine-torches were carried),
shouting the ritual Bacchic cry, *Euoi!*

than exile from this land with no harm to himself;[33]
but if he knows the murderer is someone else,   230
or from elsewhere, then let him not be silent; I'll
pay him due profit and he'll have my thanks besides.
But if you do keep silent, if somebody fearing
for a friend, or for himself, does thrust aside
my words, in that case, you must hear what I shall do: 235
I solemnly prohibit anyone within
this land whose power and throne I wield to take him in—
the man who did this—or address him, or allow
him to participate in prayers or sacrifices
to the gods, or let him share the lustral water;[34]   240
no, all must thrust him from their homes, since it is he
who is the source of our pollution, as the god's
Pythian oracle has just revealed to me.
This is the kind of ally I shall be, then, both
to the divinity and to the man who died.   245
[I pray too that the perpetrator, whether it's
one person we are unaware of, or a group,
may evilly wear out his doomed and evil life.
I also pray that if he shares my hearth and home,
with my own knowledge, I myself may suffer these   250
same curses I have just called down on other heads.[35]]
    I do enjoin you to fulfill all this
for me, and for the god, and for this land that has
been wasted so by god-forsaken fruitlessness.
For even if this matter were not sent by god,   255
it still would not befit you to leave it uncleansed—

---

33 The sense is obscure here (a line may be missing). But it seems clear
    that Oidipous is promising anyone who is secretly guilty of the
    murder that if he comes forward he will be exiled rather than killed
    in punishment.

34 Family sacrifices began with the head of the household dipping a brand
    from the altar in water, and sprinkling the assembled company. The
    presence of a guilty person at a sacrifice might render it inauspicious.
    By excluding any such person from sacrifice, the proclamation excom-
    municates him or her from the life of the household and from the shared
    cultural ties of religion.

35 Some editors delete these lines, which mar the rhetoric of the speech
    and are redundant after 236-43. Others reorganize the order of the lines
    to make the speech more coherent.

when he who perished was the best of men, and more,
your king—but to investigate it; as it is,
since it is I who now enjoy his former rule,
who share the sowing of his marriage bed and wife,   260
and would have shared in children from a common womb,
had his descendants not been so unfortunate—
but as it is, ill-fortune leaped upon his head.
I therefore shall take up this fight on his behalf
as if he were my father, and pursue all paths   265
seeking to catch the murderer of Laios, son
of Labdakos the child of Polydoros, son
of ancient Kadmos and Agenor long ago.[36]
   For those who don't do what I say, I pray the gods
may raise no crops up from their land, no children from   270
their women; may they go on being wasted by
our present destiny or one more hateful still.
As for you other Kadmeans, to whom these words
are pleasing, may both Justice, fighting as your ally,
and all the gods be with you always for the best.   275

CHORUS

I'll speak, my lord, as someone subject to your curse:
It was not I who killed him; nor can I point out
the killer. It was Phoibos' task—who sent us to
seek out this thing—to tell us who performed the deed.

OIDIPOUS

Your words are just. But no man can impose upon   280
the gods necessity to do things they don't want.

CHORUS

Then I would tell you what I think is second-best.

OIDIPOUS

If there's a third as well, don't leave your thoughts untold.

CHORUS

I know the lord whose vision is the closest to Lord
Phoibos is Teiresias; look into this   285
with his help, lord, and you'll most clearly learn the truth.

---

36 Oidipous unwittingly recites his own line of descent—a line that has
   not, as he thinks, been wiped out by the "ill-fortune" of extinction, but
   cursed with misfortune of a very different kind.

OIDIPOUS

I've not been sluggish in this action either; for
at Kreon's prompting I have sent two messengers
to bring him. I'm surprised he's not already here.

CHORUS

Aside from him, what others say is faint and old.   290

OIDIPOUS

What's this they say? I'm looking into every word.

CHORUS

It's said that he was killed by certain travellers.

OIDIPOUS

I heard that too. But no one saw who did the deed.

CHORUS

If he's susceptible to dread at all, and hears
the kind of curses you pronounced, he won't stand firm.   295

OIDIPOUS

The deed did not appall him: he won't fear mere words.

*[Enter Teiresias, a blind old prophet, led by a boy and guided by Oidipous'
attendants, along the side-entrance leading from the city.]*

CHORUS

The man is present who will show him up; these men
are leading here the godlike prophet; he's the only
human in whom truth is naturally inborn.

OIDIPOUS

Teiresias, surveyor of all things—those taught   300
and those unspoken, heavenly and walking on
the earth—although you cannot see, you understand
the sickness present in our city; we can find
no champion and no savior from it, but for you.
Phoibos—in case you haven't heard report of this—   305
sent us this answer, when we sent to ask him: that
we'll be released from this great sickness only if
we learn in full who Laios' killers are, and then
kill them or send them forth in exile from the land.
Don't grudge us the prophetic voice of birds or any   310
other road of divination that you have;[37]

---

37 Observation of the behavior and song of birds was one of the most
    important forms of divination in ancient Greek religion. Another

rescue yourself, rescue this city, rescue me
from this whole taint now emanating from the dead.
We're in your hands; the finest task is for a man
to help with every resource lying in his power.   315

TEIRESIAS

Woe! Woe! How awful to have understanding yet
not benefit from it. I knew this all too well
but it escaped me—otherwise I'd not have come.

OIDIPOUS

What is it? How down-heartedly you have arrived!

TEIRESIAS

Let me go home. If you're persuaded by me you   320
will bear your lot most easily, and I bear mine.

OIDIPOUS

It is not lawful to withhold your voice, nor is
it friendly to this city that has nurtured you.

TEIRESIAS

But I see *your* words also going somewhere quite
inopportune.[38] May I not suffer that as well!   325

OIDIPOUS

If you have understanding, by the gods, don't turn
away, since we all bow to you as suppliants.

TEIRESIAS

You all lack understanding, that is why. I won't
reveal my evils ever—not to call them yours.[39]

OIDIPOUS

What did you say? You know but will not tell? Is your   330
intention to betray us and destroy the city?

---

was examination of the remains of burnt sacrifical victims. A vivid
description of both kinds of ritual, in a failed form, is given by Teiresias
in *Antigone* (999-1014). For a discussion of Greek attitudes towards
prophets and oracles see Essay, pp. 106-7.

38 Though Oidipous' edict is for the health of the city, it will produce
"inopportune," i.e. disastrous, results for himself. Teiresias does not
wish to be the one to reveal this outcome.

39 They are Teiresias' evils because he is the only one who has knowledge
of them, but he does not wish to reveal the extent to which they are
really Oidipous' own evils.

TEIRESIAS

    I shall not grieve myself or you. Why question me
    in vain? You will discover nothing by this means.

OIDIPOUS

    Oh evilest of evil men, you'd drive the nature
    of a rock to temper! Won't you ever speak,   335
    but show yourself so rigid and intractable?

TEIRESIAS

    You criticize my temper, but you don't perceive
    the one you're dwelling with—that's why you're blaming me.[40]

OIDIPOUS

    Indeed! Who would not lose his temper hearing words
    like these, with which you're now dishonoring this city?   340

TEIRESIAS

    Though I veil things in silence, they will come themselves.

OIDIPOUS

    If they are on their way, should you not speak of them?

TEIRESIAS

    I'll tell no more. Rage back at me, if that is what
    you want, with all the savage temper that you can.

OIDIPOUS

    All right then! I'm in such a temper that I'll leave   345
    out nothing that I understand. Know that I think
    you are the one who helped conceive this deed, yes, and
    performed it, all but killing him with your own hands;
    if you had sight, I'd say the deed was yours alone.

TEIRESIAS

    Oh really? Then I tell you to abide by your   350
    own proclamation, and from this day forward speak
    no more to these people or me, since it is you
    who are the sacrilegious curse upon this land.

OIDIPOUS

    Is this the story you've so shamelessly stirred up?
    How do you think you will escape the consequences?   355

---

40 Overtly, Teiresias is referring to Oidipous' own bad temper, which can be
    thought of as "living with" him; covertly, however, his wording alludes
    to Jokasta, of whose true identity Oidipous is ignorant.

TEIRESIAS
I have escaped them, for I nurse the strength of truth.
OIDIPOUS
Truth taught by whom? Not, certainly, by your own skills.
TEIRESIAS
By you; you urged me to speak out against my will.
OIDIPOUS
Speak what? Repeat it, so that I may learn some more.
TEIRESIAS
Did you not understand before? Is this a test?   360
OIDIPOUS
Not so that I could say I know it; speak again.
TEIRESIAS
I say that that man's killer, whom you seek, is you.
OIDIPOUS
You won't be happy that you voiced disaster twice!
TEIRESIAS
Shall I add something more, to make your temper worse?
OIDIPOUS
As much as you desire; it shall be said in vain.   365
TEIRESIAS
I say you're unaware your dearest ties are most
disgraceful, and don't see what evil you are in.
OIDIPOUS
You think you'll always say this with impunity?
TEIRESIAS
Yes, if there's any power in the strength of truth.
OIDIPOUS
There is—for all but you; it is not yours because   370
you're blind in ears and mind as well as in your eyes.
TEIRESIAS
You miserable man, insulting me with taunts
with which each person here will shortly insult you.
OIDIPOUS
You nursling of unbroken night, never could you
harm me or any other man who sees the light.   375

TEIRESIAS

It's not your destiny to fall through me; Apollo
is enough; to do this deed is his concern.

OIDIPOUS

And whose 'discoveries' were these? Kreon's perhaps?[41]

TEIRESIAS

Kreon does not bring you disaster: that is you.

OIDIPOUS

Oh wealth! Oh kingly rule! Oh skill surpassing skill   380
in the competitive and highly envied life—
how great is the resentment stored in you,[42] if it's
for this, my rule—something the city placed into
my hands as an unasked-for gift—for this that he,
the trusty Kreon, he who always was my friend,   385
has crept against me secretly, desiring to
depose me, sneaking in this conjuror, this scheme-
weaving deceptive beggar-priest with eyes only
for profit, blind in using his prophetic skill.
Tell me, when have your prophecies been clear and true?   390
Why did you not, when the song-weaving hound was here,[43]
say anything to bring these townspeople release?
And yet her riddle was not one to be explained
by some man passing by—it needed prophecy,
knowledge that you conspicuously failed to get   395
from birds or any god. But then I came along,

---

41 As an absolute king, Oidipous is easily suspicious of plots against
    himself, but his choice of Kreon as a suspect is not entirely implausible
    (Essay, p. 109).

42 The "skill surpassing skill" refers to the supreme skills needed to
    be a successful ruler, but also reminds us more specifically of the
    special intelligence that sets Oidipous apart from other mortals. The
    "competitive and highly envied life" alludes to a model of heroism
    prevalent in Greek culture, whereby individuals sought to outstrip each
    other in performing exploits and gaining public honors, power and
    renown. It was assumed that others would both emulate and envy the
    most successful competitors.

43 This may reflect a mythic variant in which the Sphinx partly resembles a
    dog. Alternatively, she may be called a "hound" because she is the agent
    or servant of an angry god (in this case Hera, who had been dishonored
    by the Thebans). Similarly, the Furies (goddesses of revenge) are often
    represented as bloodhounds.

know-nothing Oidipous,[44] and brought an end to her,
succeeding by the power of thought—not taught by birds.
And I'm the man you're now attempting to depose,
because you think that you'll stand close to Kreon's throne.   400
You will, I think, bewail your purge—both you and he
who hatched this plot.[45] Did you not seem to me too old,
you'd learn by suffering what kind of thoughts yours are.

CHORUS

It seems to us, as we surmise, that both his words
and yours were spoken in a temper, Oidipous.   405
We do not need such talk: we need to look into
how best we may resolve the oracles from god.

TEIRESIAS

You may be king, but I've an equal right to answer
equally; in this I too have power, since I
live not as your slave, but as that of Loxias;[46]   410
so I do not depend on Kreon's patronage.[47]
And I say this—since you insulted me as blind:
you're sighted, but don't see what evil you are in,
or where you dwell, or who lives with you in your house.
Do you know where you come from? You are unaware   415
that you're an enemy to your own kin both under
and upon the earth; your father's and your mother's
two-pronged curse with awful foot will one day drive
you from this land in darkness, though you now see straight.[48]

---

44 Oidipous here puns explicitly on the fanciful derivation of his name from
    the Greek verb 'to know' (Essay, p. 98). His sarcastic self-description is in
    fact the essential truth about the present state of his self-knowledge.

45 For the political overtones of the word translated 'purge' see Essay
    p. 96.

46 Loxias is a common name for Apollo. Though its etymology is disputed,
    the ancient Greeks associated it with a word meaning 'oblique,' and
    thus with Apollo's oracular evasiveness.

47 By alluding to the need for foreign residents in Athens to be represented
    in legal matters by a native patron, Sophocles subtly distinguishes
    Teiresias from Oidipous, who arrived in Thebes as a supposed foreigner.
    The word originally means "defender" or "champion" (as it is translated
    at 304, 882).

48 The personified curse is one of the identities of the Furies, goddesses
    of revenge. Here they are likened to a two-pronged whip, consisting in
    curses from Oidipous' two parents.

What place won't serve as harbor to your screaming! What   420
Cithaeron won't resound with it,[49] when you have come
to realize what kind of wedding-anchorage
you sailed into within this house, ending a voyage
that had been fortunate. Nor do you realize
another crowd of evils will equate you with   425
you and your children.[50] *Now* fling mud at Kreon and
at me for speaking, since no mortal who exists
will ever be wiped out more evilly than you.

OIDIPOUS

Is it endurable to hear these words from him?
To hell with you! Get out of here at once! Go back   430
to where you came from! Just be gone and quit my house!

TEIRESIAS

I would not be here if you had not called for me.

OIDIPOUS

I didn't know that you'd speak foolishness, or I'd
scarcely have sent for you to come here to my house.

TEIRESIAS

I was born foolish—so you think; but those who brought   435
about your birth, your parents, thought I understood.

OIDIPOUS

What parents? Stay! What mortal brought about my birth?[51]

TEIRESIAS

This day will give you birth—and will destroy you too.

OIDIPOUS

The words you speak are all too riddling and unclear!

TEIRESIAS

Are you not best by birth at finding out such things?   440

OIDIPOUS

Insult me in those matters where you'll find me great!

49 Cithaeron is a mountain near Thebes. The name is used here to evoke
    mountains generally, but it also has special significance for Oidipous'
    story (Essay, p. 124).
50 On the meaning of this line see Essay p. 103. Some editors prefer to alter
    the text to a word meaning "wipe out" instead of "equate."
51 Teiresias' apparently casual mention of Oidipous' parents evidently
    strikes a nerve, reminding him of the insult directed at his legitimacy back
    in Corinth (779-80). On the "riddle" of the next line, see Essay p. 104.

TEIRESIAS
And yet that self-same fortune has destroyed you too.[52]

OIDIPOUS
I'm not concerned, if I have kept this city safe.

TEIRESIAS
Well then, I'll go.

[He turns to the boy who led him in.]
        You, child, take me away from here.

OIDIPOUS
Yes, let him take you; here beneath my feet you're making   445
trouble. Go, so that you give me no more grief.

TEIRESIAS
I'll go—when I have said the things I came for, with
no dread before your face; you can't destroy me, no!
I say to you: the man you have been seeking for
so long, with threats and proclamations in regard   450
to Laios' murder—he is here; he's said to be
a foreign resident, but soon he'll be revealed
as Theban-born; this circumstance will not be pleasing
to him: he will travel to a foreign land, now blind
instead of sighted, begging, he who was a wealthy   455
man, using a staff to point the way ahead.
He'll be revealed as living with his children as
brother and father both at once; both son and husband
of the woman who gave birth to him; his father's
fellow-sower and his murderer.[53] Go in   460
and count this up, and if you find me false, *then* say
I have no understanding from my prophet's skill.

*[Exeunt Teiresias, led by the boy along the entry-ramp by which he entered,
Oidipous into the palace. The chorus now sing and dance the first stasimon
('song in position')]*

CHORUS
        Who is the man the prophetic rock   *Strophe A*
        at Delphi sang of as having fulfilled

---

52 I.e. if Oidipous had not solved the riddle of the Sphinx, he would not
    be in the present situation.
53 I.e. both he and Laios "sowed" their seed in the same woman: Oidipous'
    mother Jokasta.

the most unspeakable of deeds   465
unspeakable with bloody hands?[54]
The hour has come for him to ply in flight
feet stronger than those of storm-swift horses;
for the offspring of Zeus,
armed with fire and lightning,   470
is leaping on him,
and the unerring, awesome Keres follow after.[55]

A voice just appearing   *Antistrophe A*
shone out from snowy Parnassus
that all should track down this mysterious man.   475
He is ranging through savage forests,
in caves and over rocks,
like a bull limping crippled
with wretched foot,[56]
trying to keep at a distance the oracles   480
from earth's navel;[57]
but they fly around him, ever-living.

With awe he shakes me, with awe,   *Strophe B*
the clever diviner of bird-signs;
I cannot accept what he says, or deny it—   485
I'm at a loss what to say.
I flutter with expectations,[58]
unable to see what is present

54 Apollo's temple at Delphi was built on a platform of rock.
55 The offspring of Zeus is Apollo, who is here serving as his father's agent
    (above, n. on 153), and armed with the latter's characteristic weapon.
    The Keres are winged goddesses of death and revenge, similar to the
    Furies and sometimes identified with them.
56 An alternative interpretation of this line is "bereft of companionship,
    wretched, with wretched foot." The interpretation given in the
    translation ties the image closely to that of the crippled Oidipous. On
    the image see further Essay, p. 110.
57 Delphi was traditionally regarded as the location of the center of the
    earth, which was marked by a large rounded stone in Apollo's temple
    called the "navel-stone."
58 'Expectation' translates the Greek *elpis*. This word is usually rendered
    in English as 'hope,' but in Greek it is an ambiguous term, referring
    to apprehensions as well as hopes about the future (compare 772 and
    see *Ant.* 615-19).

or what lies behind my back.[59]
For I have never learned, in the past or present,   490
of any quarrel in existence
between the Labdakids
and the son of Polybos,
to use as a touchstone in going against
Oidipous' repute among all the people,   495
and helping the Labdakids
with these mysterious deaths.[60]

Zeus and Apollo have understanding   *Antistrophe B*
and knowledge of mortal affairs;
among men, though, there's no true way to judge   500
if a prophet is worth more than I am myself.
A man may outstrip cleverness
with cleverness of his own.[61]
But I for one will never assent
to his critics before I see   505
their words stand up straight.
For this much was clearly revealed:
the winged maiden came at him,
and he was seen openly as clever,
and sweet for the city by that touchstone.[62]   510
Never, then, shall the verdict
of my thinking convict him of evil.

59 Since we cannot see the future, it is often represented in Greek as lying *behind* us, rather than ahead.
60 I.e. if the chorus knew of a pre-existing quarrel between the families of Laios and Polybos this might give Teiresias' accusations some credibility, and give themselves a criterion (or "touchstone") for doubting Oidipous' reputation as favorable to Thebes. This would in turn encourage them to "help" the Labdakids (i.e. the family of Laios, son of Labdakos) to solve the mysterious murder by pursuing the prophet's accusation of Oidipous. Note that although Polybos is Oidipous' adopted Corinthian father, the chorus has no reason to doubt that he is his natural father, which would make him unrelated to the Labdakids.
61 These words suggest two opposed possibilities: that the supreme intelligence of Oidipous surpasses all others (cf. 380-81), and that the special wisdom of the prophet, though not based on rational intelligence, may surpass even the king's.
62 The "winged maiden" is the Sphinx, who had the face of a woman and the body of a winged lion (Introduction, p. 18).

[Enter Kreon, along the entry-ramp leading from the city.]

KREON

    Men of the city, I am here because I heard
    that Oidipous the king has spoken awful words
    of accusation at me, which I won't endure.   515
    For if he thinks that in the present circumstances
    he has suffered something harmful at my hands,
    in word or deed, then I no longer yearn to live
    a lengthy life, if I must bear such ill-repute.
    Such words are damaging to me, not in a simple   520
    way but in the greatest sense, if I'm called evil
    in the city, and by you and by my friends.

CHORUS

    That insult did emerge from him—perhaps forced out
    by temper, not from understanding or from thought.

KREON

    Did he declare that it was by my thinking that   525
    the prophet was persuaded to assert false claims?

CHORUS

    He did; but I don't know what thinking prompted it.

KREON

    When he accused me, did his eyes look straight, and did
    the charges come from a straight-thinking mind?

CHORUS

    I don't know; I don't see what powerful people do.   530
    But here he comes himself, emerging from the house.

[Enter Oidipous from the palace.]

OIDIPOUS

    You there! How could you come here? Is your face so bold
    that you have dared to come here to my house, when you
    are clearly both the murderer of this man here,
    and robber of my kingdom in the eyes of all?[63]   535
    Come, tell me, by the gods, was it because you viewed
    me as a fool or coward that you made these plans?

---

63 "This man here" is a common Greek idiom for referring to oneself (Essay, pp. 96-7). In calling Kreon his "murderer" and "robber," Oidipous is, of course, exaggerating (though cf. 669-70). But his choice of language also equates Kreon with Laios' murderer (cf. 122, 124).

Or did you think I'd not find out about your deed
as it sneaked up on me, or if I learned of it
would not protect myself? Is not your task a foolish   540
one, to hunt for kingship without wealth or friends,
when catching it needs property and mass support?

KREON

You know what you should do? Listen to equal words
in answer to your own; then judge, when you have learned.

OIDIPOUS

Your speaking skill is awesome, but I'm slow to learn—   545
from *you*, since you're a hostile burden, so I've found.

KREON

First hear what I shall say upon this very point.

OIIPOUS

Upon this very point, don't tell me you're not evil.

KREON

If you believe that wilfulness without good sense
is something worth possessing, you're not thinking straight.   550

OIDIPOUS

If *you* believe that you can harm a kinsman and
not pay the penalty, then you're not thinking well.[64]

KREON

Those words were justly spoken, I agree; but tell
me what this suffering you say you've suffered *is*.

OIDIPOUS

Did you, or did you not, persuade me that I should   555
send someone for the reverent man of prophecy?

KREON

I did; and I still think this was the proper plan.

OIDIPOUS

How long a time has passed since this man Laios went...

KREON

And did what kind of deed? I do not understand.

OIDIPOUS

...and vanished from your sight, struck by a deadly blow?   560

---

64 These two lines, like many others, refer ironically to Oidipous himself,
    who will, of course, himself pay for mistreating his closest kin.

KREON

You'd have to measure out a long and ancient time.

OIDIPOUS

And back then was this prophet practising his skill?

KREON

As cleverly as now, and honored equally.

OIDIPOUS

And did he mention me at all, at that time then?

KREON

No; not at least at any time when I stood by.   565

OIDIPOUS

But did you not inquire then who the killer was?

KREON

We did, of course, but did not hear of anything.

OIDIPOUS

If he's so clever, why did he not speak out then?

KREON

I don't know; I keep silent when I lack sound thought.

OIDIPOUS

But this you do know, and, if thinking well, would say.[65]   570

KREON

What's that? If I do know, I won't refuse to speak.

OIDIPOUS

That were he not in league with you, he never would
have said it was by me that Laios was destroyed.

KREON

You know if that is what he said. But I've the right
to learn these things from you as much as you from me.   575

OIDIPOUS

Learn then—you won't convict *me* as a murderer.

KREON

All right: do you not have my sister as your wife?

OIDIPOUS

That statement is impossible to contradict.

---

65 On the ambiguity of expressions meaning "good thinking" see Essay
   p. 105.

KREON

And in your rule, do you not give her equal power?[66]

OIDIPOUS

Yes; anything she ever wants, she gets from me.   580

KREON

And as a third, am I not equal to you both?

OIDIPOUS

Exactly; that's what shows you are an evil friend.

KREON

Not if you argue with yourself as I have done.
Consider, first, if you think anyone would choose
to rule in fear instead of sleeping peacefully—   585
provided that his power's the same. It's not my nature
to desire to be a king when I can act
already like a king, nor is it that of any
other man who knows how to be sensible.
Now I gain all things fearlessly from you; were I   590
the ruler, I would often have to act against
my will.[67] How then could kingship be a sweeter
thing for me to have than painless rule and royal
power? I'm not so self-deceived that I desire
to have more than what is both fine and profits me.   595
Now everyone is glad to see me, now I am
embraced by everyone, now those desiring things
from you seek me out, since success depends on me.
Why then would I exchange this way of life for yours?
A mind that's sound could not become an evil one.   600
I'm not in love with thinking of that kind, nor could
I bear to act that way in league with someone else.
Test me: go back to Delphi and inquire if my
report about the oracle was clear and true;
then, if you catch me having shared in any plan   605
with the diviner, take me off and kill me, not

66 Oidipous and Jokasta are not joint rulers, but as his wife he consults
    her and grants her authority equivalent to his own. Kreon's emphasis
    on equality is not a constitutional fact, but a rhetorical ploy to set up
    the following argument.

67 Although an absolute ruler can in principle do whatever he wants, a
    responsible king will often be constrained by the needs and wishes
    of his people.

by one vote, but by two: my own as well as yours.
But don't accuse me without evidence, with unclear
judgment. It's unjust to think without due cause
that evil men are good, or good men evil ones.   610
To cast a good friend out, I say, is equal to
rejecting what one loves the most—one's very life.[68]
As time goes by you will securely recognize
all this; for only time points out the just; but you
may recognize who's evil in a single day.[69]   615

CHORUS

He's spoken well for someone careful not to fall,
my lord; fast thinking does not bring security.

OIDIPOUS

When someone making plans against me secretly
moves fast, I must be fast to make my counter-plans.
If I remain inactive, this man's schemes will be   620
accomplished, my mistakes irrevocably made.

KREON

What then is your desire? To cast me from the land?

OIDIPOUS

Far from it! I don't want your exile, but your death!
* * * * * * * * * *

KREON

When you point out what kind of thing resentment is...[70]
* * * * * * * * * *

OIDIPOUS

You speak as if you won't believe my words and yield.   625

KREON

No, for I see you thinking badly.

---

68 This sentiment draws on two commonplaces of Greek friendship:
    one's self (or soul, or life) is one's closest friend, and a true friend
    is a "second self."

69 Kreon's central point is that with time his innocence will be revealed.
    The antithetical statement, that bad people are often quickly revealed
    by some word or deed, is strictly irrelevant in this context, but applies
    ironically to the case of Oidipous himself (cf. 438 and Essay p. 104).

70 This line makes little sense in context. Some editors posit one or more
    lines before or after it which have fallen out of the manuscripts.

OIDIPOUS
Well for me!

KREON
You should think equally of me.

OIDIPOUS
You're evil-born.

KREON
What if you do not understand?

OIDIPOUS
Yet I must rule!71

KREON
Not if your rule's an evil one.

OIDIPOUS
Oh city, city!

KREON
The city's not just yours: I share in it as well.   630

CHORUS
Stop this, my lords! I see Jokasta opportunely
coming from the house; with her arrival you
should set to rights the quarrel that has just flared up.

[Enter Jokasta from the palace.]

JOKASTA
What is this foolish verbal strife, you wretches, which
you have provoked? Aren't you ashamed of stirring up   635
these private evils when the land itself's so sick?
You, go into the house, and Kreon, you to yours;
don't turn what's nothing into some great cause of grief.

KREON
Blood-sister, Oidipous your husband thinks it right
to do to me one of two awful evil things: 640
to thrust me from my fatherland or have me killed.72

OIDIPOUS
Yes, wife; for I have caught him doing evil deeds
against my person with the aid of evil skills.

---

71 Alternatively, this could mean "you must obey."
72 The text here is probably corrupt, but the sense must be something like
    that given in the translation.

KREON

May I not prosper! May I perish, cursed, if I
have done to you one thing that you accuse me of!   645

JOKASTA

I beg you by the gods, believe him, Oidipous,
respecting most of all his oath sworn by the gods,
but also me and all these people present here.[73]

*[The chorus and actors now participate in a kommos, or lyric
dialogue, interspersed with trimeters (649-96).]*

CHORUS

My lord, take thought, be willing   *Strophe*
to be persuaded, I beseech you—   650

OIDIPOUS

In what do you want me to yield?

CHORUS

Respect this man; in the past he was no fool,
and now he is made mighty by his oath.

OIDIPOUS

You know what you desire?

CHORUS

                              I know.

OIDIPOUS

                                        Explain your words.

CHORUS

Don't cast off a friend in dishonor, one bound by a curse, 655
with an unproven verbal accusation.

OIDIPOUS

Know well that when you seek for this, you're seeking for
my own destruction or my exile from this land.

CHORUS

No, by Helios, god
foremost of all gods![74]   660

---

73 Although Kreon did not mention the gods explicitly, the powerful
   curse under which he has placed himself implies their sanction. It
   was customary in Athenian trials to swear an oath to one's own
   innocence.

74 Helios, the sun god, is also an important god of oaths because in his
   journey across the sky he sees all things and is therefore aware of

May I perish forsaken
by gods and friends
in the greatest extremity,
if such is my thinking!
But alas for me, ill-fated,   665
the land, decaying, tears my heart,
if this quarrel between you two
is to join our ancient evils.

OIDIPOUS

Then he may go—even if I must utterly
die or be thrust, dishonored, from this land by force.   670
I feel compassion for your piteous request—
not his; *him* I'll abhor, wherever he may be.

KREON

Yielding's abhorrent to you, clearly; when you're so
far gone in rage you're burdensome. Such natures are
most grievous for themselves to bear, and justly so.   675

OIDIPOUS

Get out of here! Leave me alone!

KREON

                          I'm on my way.
I've found you ignorant: these people kept me safe.

[Exit Kreon along the entry-way leading to the city.]

CHORUS

Woman, why do you delay   *Antistrophe*
to take this man into the house?

JOKASTA

I will after learning what fortune occurred.   680

CHORUS

An ignorant verbal suspicion arose;
and such injustice tears the heart.

JOKASTA

This came from both of them?

CHORUS

                          It did.

---

anyone who commits perjury. He is here called "foremost" of the gods
because of his importance in this capacity.

JOKASTA

And what was said?

CHORUS

It seems to me enough, with the land in mind,
enough, for this to rest where it broke off.[75]   685

OIDIPOUS

You see where you have come to, excellent in judgment
though you are, trying to dull my heart's keen edge?

CHORUS

My lord, know this—
I've said it more than once—
that I would be revealed   690
to be out of my mind,
resourceless in sound thought,
if I kept my distance from you—
you who, when my dear land
was frantic with despair,   695
wafted it back on a straight course.
Now may you again be our good guide!

JOKASTA

Tell me too, by the gods, my lord, the matter that
has caused you to establish and retain such wrath.

OIDIPOUS

I'll speak; for I revere you more than these folk, wife.   700
It's Kreon, and the plans against me that he's hatched.

JOKASTA

Speak clearly of the quarrel that you blame him for.

OIDIPOUS

He says the murderer of Laios is myself.

JOKASTA

He knows this for himself, or taught by someone else?

OIDIPOUS

Neither. He sent an evil-working prophet here,   705

---

75 This concern for the land is the play's last allusion to the plague. As
the circle draws in on Oidipous, identifying him as the cause of the
land's sickness, the sufferings of the Thebans become more narrowly
projected onto him as an individual, and references to "the city"
markedly decrease.

and so he keeps his own mouth fully free from blame.

JOKASTA
Release yourself from fear about the matters that
you're speaking of. Listen to me and learn that there's
no mortal creature sharing in prophetic skill.
I shall reveal to you brief evidence of this: 710
An oracle once came to Laios—I won't say
from Phoibos, but from Phoibos' servants—saying that
his destiny would be to perish at the hand
of any child that would be born to him and me.
And yet, the story goes, some foreign robbers killed   715
him one day at a junction where three highways meet;[76]
as for our child, three days had not passed since his birth
when Laios yoked his feet and had him thrown, at someone
else's hand, on the untrodden mountainside.[77]
So Phoibos did not bring to pass that he should be   720
his father's murderer, or Laios suffer at
his own child's hand—the awful thing he feared; yet this
is what the words of prophecy marked out for them.
So pay them no attention; if a god seeks what
he needs, he'll easily uncover it himself.   725

OIDIPOUS
What wandering of spirit, wife, has gripped me since
I heard you speak just now—what turbulence of thought!

JOKASTA
What anxious thought arrests you and inspires these words?

OIDIPOUS
Here's what I thought I heard you saying: Laios was
slaughtered right at a junction where three highways meet.   730

JOKASTA
Yes—that is what was said, nor has the rumor ceased.

OIDIPOUS
Where is this spot at which he suffered such a thing?

---

76 For the symbolic significance of this famous junction see Essay, pp. 114-5.
    The word translated "story" (*phatis*) is also used for prophetic "voices"
    at 151, 310, 322, 1440, and for Oidipous' reputation at 495.

77 In some versions of the tale, the infant Oidipous is pinned through
    the ankles, but Sophocles' wording implies nothing more specific
    than feet.

JOKASTA

The land's called Phocis, and the place is where the road
forks, leading folk from Delphi and from Daulia.

OIDIPOUS

And how much time has passed since the event occurred?   735

JOKASTA

The city heard the proclamation just before
you were revealed to us as ruler of this land.

OIDIPOUS

Oh Zeus, what have you planned to do regarding me?

JOKASTA

What is this, Oidipous, that so disturbs your heart?

OIDIPOUS

Don't ask me yet; but tell me more of Laios—what   740
was his physique, and was he still in manhood's prime?

JOKASTA

His hair was dark, just blooming with a sheen of white;
and in appearance he was not too far from you.

OIDIPOUS

Alas, wretch that I am! It seems I have just cast
an awful curse upon myself in ignorance.   745

JOKASTA

What do you mean? I shudder as I gaze at you!

OIDIPOUS

My heart fears awfully the prophet may have sight.
Say one more thing, and you will point me to the truth.

JOKASTA

I shudder, but I'll speak—when I learn what you ask.

OIDIPOUS

Did he proceed with few attending him, or with   750
the kind of retinue that suits a ruling man?

JOKASTA

The group was five in number altogether, one
a herald; and a single carriage carried Laios.[78]

---

78 The herald is mentioned because he would have been a conspicuous
    member of the party, bearing a herald's staff and preceeding the king's
    carriage (he is the "leader" referred to at 804).

OIDIPOUS

Aiai! These things are now transparent! Tell me, wife,
who was the person who reported this to you?   755

JOKASTA

The only one who got back safely: a house-slave.

OIDIPOUS

Tell me, is he by chance still present in the house?

JOKASTA

No longer. When he came back here and saw that you
were holding power, and Laios dead, he touched my hand
in supplication, begging me to send him to   760
the countryside to pasture flocks, so that he might
be out of sight of town as far as possible.
I sent him; since he was deserving, for a slave,
to win this favor or an even greater one.

OIDIPOUS

Then how can he return here quickly, back to us?   765

JOKASTA

That can be done. But what's the point of this desire?

OIDIPOUS

I'm very much afraid, my wife, that I have said
a lot too much; that's why I want to see this man.

JOKASTA

Then he shall come; but surely I deserve to learn
as well, my lord, what's causing you so much distress.   770

OIDIPOUS

I won't withold it from you, now that I have come
so far in expectation; to whom should I speak,
while going through such fortunes, better than to you?
    My father was king Polybos of Corinth and
my mother Merope, a Dorian. I was   775
thought greatest man among the townsfolk there until
some fortune brought this chance event, deserving of
surprise, but not deserving serious concern:
a man at dinner who had drunk too much called me
over the wine, a bastard, not my father's son.   780
Oppressed in spirit, I restrained myself for that
day—barely—but the next I went up to my mother
and my father and I questioned them. They came

down hard upon the fellow who had let that insult
fly; I was delighted; nonetheless the thing   785
kept nagging at me; for the tale spread far and wide.
So then I made my way to Pytho, secretly
from both my mother and my father; Phoibos did
not honor the request I came with, but instead
sent me away with words revealing other awful   790
and unhappy things for miserable me:
I must have intercourse with my own mother, show
to human eyes a race unbearable to see,
and kill the father of my birth. When I heard this
I fled in exile from the land of Corinth, using
stars to measure out a path to keep me far   795
away from it in future, somewhere I should never
see the insults of these evil oracles
attain fulfilment. As I went my way, I reached
the region where you say this king of yours was killed.

    Now, wife, to you I'll speak the truth. As I came near,   800
upon my travels, to that threefold path, I met
a herald, and a man who rode upon a carriage
drawn by colts, in just the way that you described.
The two of them—the leader and the older man
himself—both tried to drive me from the road by force.[79]   805
The driver, who was trying to push me to one side—
I struck him in a temper. When the older man
saw this, he watched till I was passing by his wagon
then brought down a two-pronged goad right on my head.
The price he paid was more than equal: swiftly hit   810
by this hand with my staff, he was sent rolling headlong
from the carriage all the way onto his back.
I killed the lot of them. If any kinship tie
connects this foreigner with Laios,[80] who could now
be sunk in deeper misery than this man here?   815
What man could be more hateful to divinities,
than he whom no one, foreigner or townsman, may
address or take into his house, but rather all

79 The road here ran through a steep, narrow, wooded valley, down which
    Oidipous was descending while Laios' party drove up it (cf. 1398-9).
80 "This foreigner" refers overtly to the man in the carriage, but on an
    ironic level it might be taken to refer to Oidipous himself.

must thrust him from their homes. And it is I myself—
none other—who has laid this curse upon myself.   820
And with the same two hands that killed him I am now
fouling the dead man's marriage-bed. Am I not evil
in my birth, yes, utterly impure, if I
must flee to exile, and yet never see my kin
or step into my fatherland, or else I must   825
be yoked in marriage to my mother, kill my father
Polybos, who nurtured me and gave me birth?
Would someone not speak rightly of this man if he
should judge that it was some savage divinity
who sent me this? Oh never, you pure reverence of   830
the gods, oh never may I see that day! No, may
I disappear from mortal sight before I see
the stain of such dire circumstances come on me.

CHORUS
This makes us shudder, lord; but cling to hope until
you learn what happened from the person who was there.   835

OIDIPOUS
Indeed this is the only scrap of hope that's left
for me, to wait until that man, the herdsman, comes.

JOKASTA
What is your heart's desire for him, when he appears?

OIDIPOUS
I'll tell you: if he's found to give the same account
as you, then I will have escaped from suffering.   840

JOKASTA
What did you hear me say that was remarkable?

OIDIPOUS
You said he spoke of *men* who killed him, robbers in
the plural; if that's still the number that he says,
I'm not the killer: many cannot equal one.   845
But if he clearly mentions one man traveling
alone, the balance of the deed then tilts my way.[81]

81 The metaphor is one of a sinking pan on a scale, like the scales that
    Zeus uses in the *Iliad* to determine which of two duelling warriors is
    fated to die (e.g. 22.209-13). In this case it suggests both the weight
    of accumulating evidence, and the burden of responsibility weighing
    down on Oidipous' head (compare *Ant.* 1346-7).

JOKASTA

Know well this *is* the way his story was revealed;
it is impossible that he disown it now,
since all the city heard these things, not me alone.   850
But even if he deviates from what he said
back then, never will he reveal that it is true,
my lord, that Laios' murder was predicted right,[82]
for Loxias expressly said that he must die
at my son's hands; yet it was never my unhappy   855
child that killed him, since the infant perished first.
Therefore, as far as prophecy's concerned, I would
in future not look this way as opposed to that.[83]

OIDIPOUS

You reason well. But all the same, send somebody
to bring the laborer—do not omit this task.   860

JOKASTA

I'll do it fast; but let's go back inside the house.
I'd not do anything that was not dear to you.

*[Exeunt into the palace. The chorus now sing and dance the second
stasimon.]*

CHORUS

May destiny be at my side   *Strophe A*
as I bear reverence and purity
in all my words and deeds,   865
under those laws set up, lofty of foot,
born in heaven's bright air,
which have no father but Olympos;[84]
the mortal nature of men did not
give them their birth, nor shall   870
forgetfulness ever put them to sleep;
the god in them is great and untouched by age.[85]

---

82 Literally, "straight" (see n. on 39).

83 These words may be an image from prophetic bird-watching (cf., n. on
    311). But it could also simply mean "I won't give prophecy the time of
    day." Jokasta is still arguing against Teiresias' credibility, rather than
    addressing the more recent evidence.

84 The chorus imagine divine laws, governing human words and deeds,
    displayed in the heavenly home of the gods (Olympus) just as the Athenian
    laws were displayed in public inscriptions (compare *Ant.* 450-57).

85 "The god" here refers to the divine power that inheres in these laws.

Outrage gives birth to kings;[86]	*Antistrophe A*
surfeited in futile folly	
with much that is inopportune,	875
disadvantageous, outrage mounts	
to the topmost pinnacle and plunges	
down necessity's precipice,	
where feet are useless.[87]	
Yet I pray that god may never break up	880
the contest that's good for the city;[88]	
never shall I cease to have god as my champion.[89]	

But if someone travels	*Strophe B*
haughtily in hand or word,[90]	
unfearful of Justice, not revering	885
the seats of divinities,	
may an evil destiny seize him	
for his ill-destined decadence,	

The use here and elsewhere of "god" in the singular, as opposed to the plural "gods," has no special significance.

86 The Greek word implies the role of the biological father rather than the mother. "Outrage" translates the Greek *hubris*, and "king" translates *turannos*. The meaning of the whole line is much disputed (see Essay pp. 118-9).

87 The personified figure of *hubris* is imagined elevating itself to the pinnacle of a roof or mountain, from which its own momentum casts it down (compare the description of Kapaneus at *Ant.* 127-40). The inability of *hubris* to use its feet suggests both a sardonic reference to falling through the air and the incapacity of someone crushed by such a fall. This is contrasted with the divine laws which are "lofty of foot" i.e. live and move effectively up in heaven.

88 The chorus here distinguishes the self-seeking of the autocrat from beneficial competitiveness, such as Oidipous' struggle to save the city of Thebes, which characterizes the successful hero and king (cf. n. on 382).

89 The connection of thought seems to be that divine approval is the factor determining whether competitive striving is beneficial or harmful. Like the corresponding line in the strophe (871), this line asserts the chorus' piety as grounds for their convictions.

90 The travel metaphor alludes generally to the "road of life;" but evokes more specifically the wanderings of Oidipous, and his encounter with Laios, which might be judged as "haughty" on either side, or both (Essay pp. 116-17). The word translated as "haughtily" literally means "overlooking"—a word applicable to Oidipous' behavior here in a different sense.

unless his profts are reaped justly
and he abstains from irreverence,   890
or if he clings in wicked folly
to what is untouchable.[91]
What man in that case will succeed
in warding off arrows of rage from his life?
For if such deeds are held in honor   895
why should I dance for the gods?[92]

I will no longer reverently go   *Antistrophe B*
to earth's untouchable navel,
or to the temple at Abai,
or that of Olympia,[93]   900
if these prophecies don't fit together
for every mortal hand to point to.
Rather, oh Zeus ruling in power,
if you are rightly so addressed,[94] lord of all,
may you and your immortal rule   905
not rest unaware of this.
For people are already dismissing
the oracles about Laios, which are decaying;
Apollo no longer stands conspicuous in honor;
and godliness has vanished.   910

[Enter Jokasta from the palace, carrying garlands and incense.]

JOKASTA
Lords of this land, the idea came to me to go
in supplication to the temples of the gods,
taking these garlands here and incense in my hands.
For Oidipous excites his heart excessively

---

91 Sacred items and places are often represented as "untouchable" by
human beings (compare 898 and *OC* 39-40).

92 Dancing was an important form of divine worship (compare 1092),
and the chorus-members are themselves dancing as they sing these
words (see Essay p. 120).

93 For the navel of the earth see above, n. on 481. Abai was a nearby town
northeast of Delphi, which also had an important oracle of Apollo.
Olympia was an major shrine and oracle of Zeus in the Peloponnese
(see Map 1).

94 I.e. Zeus must now prove the appropriateness of his title as "ruling in
power" by exercising that power on behalf of the oracles.

with painful thoughts of every kind; he does not, like   915
a man of sound mind, use old things as evidence
for new;[95] each speaker sways him—if he speaks of fear.
As I am getting nowhere by advising him,
I've come to supplicate you with these prayers, since you
are nearest, Lykeian Apollo,[96] that you may   920
provide us some release untainted by a curse;
for as things are, we shudder, all of us, to see
him stricken from his wits—the helmsman of our ship.

[Enter messenger along the entry-ramp leading from the country. He is an old, poor and low-class man, but not a slave.]

MESSENGER 1

Might I learn from you foreigners, perhaps, where stands
the house of Oidipous the king? Or best of all,   925
if you know where he is himself, then tell me that.[97]

CHORUS

This is his dwelling, foreigner, and he's inside;
this woman is his wife and mother of his children.[98]

MESSENGER 1

Then may she always prosper, and the ones she lives
with prosper too, since she is that man's wedded wife.[99]   930

JOKASTA

The same to you, for you deserve it, foreigner,
for these kind words of yours. But tell me why you've come—
what you desire, or what you're wishing to report.

95   I.e. use the oracle given to Laios, which apparently failed, as evidence
     for the unreliability of the more recent oracles given to himself. Or
     possibly, she means that the manner in which he is now using the old as
     evidence for new is not the manner of a rational man.
96   Apollo is 'nearest' in more than one sense. An altar of Apollo stood by
     the door of most houses, and may have been represented on stage. And
     Apollo is the god most closely related to the oracles in question.
97   Each of these three lines ends with a pun on the name of Oidipous as one
     who knows, plus a word for "where" (*oim' hopou, Oidipou, oisth' hopou*),
     producing a rhyming effect that is rare in Greek (cf. Essay, p. 99).
98   The ironic wording ("wife and mother…of his children") reflects that
     of the Greek.
99   The word "wedded" translates a Greek word meaning 'complete,'
     indicating that the marriage has been 'completed' by the birth of
     children. This is part of the reason for the messenger's congratulation,
     and as such, of course, bears heavy irony.

MESSENGER 1

Good tidings for your husband, woman, and your house.

JOKASTA

What kind of thing? And from what person have you come?   935

MESSENGER 1

I come from Corinth, and my tale will surely please
you—yes, of course it will. But it may grieve you too.

JOKASTA

What is it? How does it possess such double power?

MESSENGER 1

The local people of that land will set him up
as king of Isthmia—that's what they're saying there.[100]   940

JOKASTA

What? Is old Polybos no longer wielding power?

MESSENGER 1

No longer; death now holds him buried in the tomb.

JOKASTA

What's this you say? Is Oidipous' father dead?

MESSENGER 1

If I'm not speaking truly I deserve to die.

JOKASTA [to one of her attendants]

Go to your master, serving maid, and tell him this   945
as fast as possible.

[Exit servant into the palace.]

You prophecies from gods,
see where you stand now! Oidipous stayed exiled for
so long from terror that he'd kill that man; now he
has died through some chance fortune, not at this man's hand.

[Enter Oidipous from inside the palace.]

OIDIPOUS

Jokasta, dearest royal wife, why did you send   950
your maid to bring me here to you outside the house?

---

100 Isthmia is the land governed by Corinth, named for the Isthmus of
    Corinth, a narrow neck of land connecting mainland Greece to the
    Peloponnese (see Map 2).

JOKASTA

First listen to this man; when you have heard him, look
where they have gone, those reverent prophecies from god.

OIDIPOUS

Who is this man? What does he have to say to me?

JOKASTA

He comes from Corinth to report that that Polybos   955
your father is no longer living: he is dead.

OIDIPOUS

What are you saying, foreigner? Tell me yourself.

MESSENGER 1

If I must give you first a clear report of this
event, know well that he is really dead and gone.

OIDIPOUS

Destroyed by treachery, or did some sickness strike?   960

MESSENGER 1

A slight tilt sends an old man's body to its rest.[101]

OIDIPOUS

Poor wretch, he perished from some sickness, so it seems.

MESSENGER 1

That and the length of time that he had measured out.

OIDIPOUS

Alas, alas! Why should one look, then, oh my wife,
to the prophetic hearth of Pytho or the birds   965
screeching above us, whose interpreters declared
that I was going to kill my father?[102] He is dead,
concealed beneath the earth, while I am here and have
not touched my sword—unless he perished out of longing
for me; that's one way I might have caused his death.   970
In any case, the present prophecies now lie

---

101 The image is again that of a balance (compare above, n. on 847). But
"tilting" is also a medical term, referring to a slight shift in a patient's
condition.

102 The "Pythian hearth" was a hearth kept constantly alight in Apollo's
temple at Delphi, on which laurel-leaves were burned before the
priestess gave her prophecies (cf. above, n. on 32). The word "screech"
suggests that the birds' cries are unintelligible, or in this context,
meaningless (compare *Ant.* 1001)

in Hades, worthless, taken there by Polybos.[103]

JOKASTA

Is that not just what I've been saying all along?

OIDIPOUS

You said it, yes; but I was led astray by fear.

JOKASTA

From now on don't take any of these things to heart.   975

OIDIPOUS

But how should I not shudder at my mother's bed?

JOKASTA

What should a human being fear, who's in the power
of fortune and cannot know clearly what's to come?[104]
It's best to take life as it comes, as far as possible.
So don't be fearful of your mother's marriage-bed;   980
for many mortal men have shared their mother's bed
in dreams as well;[105] the person who treats all such things
as meaning nothing bears this life most easily.

OIDIPOUS

All this would be well said by you, if she who bore
me weren't alive still; as it is, she lives, so I   985
must shudder by necessity, though you speak well.

JOKASTA

Your father's funeral's a mighty ray of hope.[106]

---

103 If Polybos had died out of longing for his adopted son, then the oracle
would have been fulfilled without any responsibility on Oidipous'
part. If not, Oidipous in no way caused his father's death. Either way,
the oracle is now "dead" in the sense that its threat has supposedly
been averted.

104 I.e. since the future is unpredictable, we should not fear any specific
event that has been prophesied.

105 Dreams, as well as oracles, were regarded as omens of the future. A
dream might also be seen as an innocuous fulfilment of the oracle
(Essay pp. 106-7).

106 Literally, "a great eye." The eye was regarded as the most precious part
of the body, and was thought of as emitting a ray of light. It therefore
came to stand for the light of hope or safety (cf. 81), or anything
precious, especially a dearly-loved family-member (compare 999). The
latter meaning gives the expression extra poignance in this context,
where anxiety about the oracles has rendered the death of a close family
member joyful instead of sad.

OIDIPOUS

It is; but I still fear that woman who's alive.

MESSENGER 1

Who is this woman that you're also fearful of?

OIDIPOUS

It's Merope, old man, who lived with Polybos.   990

MESSENGER 1

And what's the reason that you have this fear of her?

OIDIPOUS

An awful god-sent prophecy, oh foreigner.

MESSENGER 1

Can it be spoken? Or may no one else be told?

OIDIPOUS

It's certainly permitted. Loxias once said
I must have intercourse with my own mother and   995
must take my father's blood with my own hands. That's why
I've made my home so far from Corinth all this time.
I have enjoyed good fortune; yet it is most sweet
to look upon the eyes of those who gave one birth.[107]

MESSENGER 1

And so you left that city shuddering at this?   1000

OIDIPOUS

I'd no desire to shed my father's blood, old man.

MESSENGER 1

Then since I've come here with good will towards you, lord,
why don't I instantly release you from this fear?

OIDIPOUS

Indeed, you'd win from me the thanks that you deserve.

MESSENGER 1

Indeed, that's mainly what I came here for, to reap   1005
some kind of benefit when you came home again.

OIDIPOUS

I'll never go to join the ones who gave me birth!

MESSENGER 1

You don't know what you're doing, child, that's very clear.

---

107 "Eyes" is often used in this way to mean "face." But in this particular
     play such expressions have a special resonance.

OIDIPOUS

How's that, old man? Tell me your meaning, by the gods.

MESSENGER 1

If on account of this you flee from going home.   1010

OIDIPOUS

I dread that Phoibos' words may turn out clear and true.

MESSENGER 1

That taint may reach you from the ones who gave you birth?

OIDIPOUS

Yes, this—this is what always frightens me, old man.

MESSENGER 1

Then do you know you're justly terrified of nothing?

OIDIPOUS

How so, if I was really born these parents' child?   1015

MESSENGER 1

Because king Polybos was not your kin at all.

OIDIPOUS

What? Was not Polybos the father of my birth?

MESSENGER 1

No more than this man here, but equally with me.

OIDIPOUS

How could a nothing equal him who gave me birth?

MESSENGER 1

Because that man begot you no more than myself.   1020

OIDIPOUS

What was his reason, then, for calling me his child?

MESSENGER 1

Know that he got you from my hands once as a gift.

OIDIPOUS

Yet he so greatly loved me—from another's hand?

MESSENGER 1

His prior childlessness persuaded him to this.

OIDIPOUS

And did you chance upon this gift, or pay for me?   1025

MESSENGER 1

I found you in Cithaeron's winding wooded glens.

OIDIPOUS

And for what reason were you traveling in those parts?

MESSENGER 1

I supervised a flock that grazed the mountainside.

OIDIPOUS

You mean you were a shepherd, wandering for hire?[108]

MESSENGER 1

And at that time, my child, I was your savior too.   1030

OIDIPOUS

What was the anguish that your hands preserved me from?

MESSENGER 1

A grief to which your feet could serve as witnesses.

OIDIPOUS

Alas, why does this ancient evil cross your lips?

MESSENGER 1

When I released you, both your feet were pierced right through.

OIDIPOUS

An awful insult picked up from my swaddling bands.[109]   1035

MESSENGER 1

From this chance fortune you were named the one you are.[110]

OIDIPOUS

Which of my parents did this? Tell me, by the gods!

MESSENGER 1

I don't know; he who gave you to me would know more.

OIDIPOUS

It was not you who chanced on me, but someone else?

---

108 The shepherd is a hired laborer, the lowest class of free person, who in the eyes of a nobleman would rank little more than a slave. Hence Oidipous' tone is one of some contempt, and the shepherd's response slightly reproachful.

109 Swaddling bands were cloths in which infants were tightly confined for about two months after birth. The expression is similar to the English "from the cradle." Ironically, the verb translated "picked up" is the same verb used for a father acknowledging the legitimacy of a new-born baby and accepting it into the family.

110 The name Oidipous was popularly supposed to be derived from two words meaning 'swollen' and 'foot' (Essay, p. 98).

MESSENGER 1

Another shepherd gave you to me as a gift.   1040

OIDIPOUS

Who was the fellow? Can you make this clear in words?

MESSENGER 1

I think that he was named as one of Laios' men.

OIDIPOUS

You mean the king who ruled this land once, long ago?

MESSENGER 1

Yes; that's the man this fellow served as herdsman for.

OIDIPOUS

And is the fellow still alive, for me to see?   1045

MESSENGER 1

You local people of this land would know that best.

OIDIPOUS

Does anyone among you know the herdsman that
he speaks of, having seen him either here or in
the countryside? If so, inform me, since the time
is opportune for all of this to be found out.   1050

CHORUS

I think he is none other than the countryman
whom you were seeking earlier to see. But she,
Jokasta here, could tell you best if that is so.

OIDIPOUS

You know that shepherd, wife, whom we just now desired
to come here? Is it he of whom this fellow speaks?   1055

JOKASTA

What of it? Pay it no attention. Do not even
wish to call to mind mere foolish, futile words.

OIDIPOUS

It is impossible that I should get such
evidence and not reveal the truth about my birth.

JOKASTA

No, by the gods! If you have any care at all for your   1060
own life, don't search this out! My sickness is enough.[111]

---

111 Jokasta uses the sickness metaphor to refer to her own distress at
perceiving the truth, but Oidipous assumes she is simply upset about
his supposed low birth.

OIDIPOUS

Take heart! If I'm revealed a triple slave, my mother
thrice enslaved, *you* won't be shown as evil-born.[112]

JOKASTA

Yet be persuaded, I beseech you—don't do this!

OIDIPOUS

You can't persuade me not to clearly learn the truth.   1065

JOKASTA

I speak the best for you—I understand things well.[113]

OIDIPOUS

This "best for you"'s been grieving me for some time now.

JOKASTA

Ill-destined, may you never find out who you are!

OIDIPOUS

Won't someone go and bring that herdsman here to me?
And let this woman here enjoy her wealthy birth.   1070

JOKASTA

Ah! Ah! Unhappy one! This is the only word
I can address you with—that's all, for evermore.

[Jokasta rushes off into the palace.]

CHORUS

Why has your wife departed from us, Oidipous,
rushing away in savage pain? I am afraid
that from her silence something evil will break forth.[114]   1075

OIDIPOUS

Break forth what will! I shall pursue my wish to see
the seed I spring from, even if its rank is small.
She may perhaps feel shame—since, like a woman, she
thinks big—to find out that I am of wretched birth.[115]

---

112 This might mean "utterly a slave," or "a third-generation slave." For the
ambiguities in the meaning of *kakos* see Essay, p. 124.

113 This is a good example of the ambiguity of *phron-* words (Essay, p. 105).
Jokasta means that she is concerned for Oidipous' well-being, but she also
understands things on an intellectual level better than he does.

114 The image is that of the calm before a storm (compare 1280). For the
dangers of such reticence in a departing character compare *Ant.* 1244-52.

115 Despite his unusually warm and intimate relationship with his wife,
Oidipous shares the general cultural contempt for women and their
concerns (see Essay, p. 123).

But *I* won't be dishonored, since I count myself   1080
a child of Fortune with her beneficial gifts.
This is the mother I was born from, and my kin
the months have marked me out to be both small and great.[116]
So born, I never could turn out to be another
person and not learn in full about my birth.   1085

[The chorus now sing and dance the brief third stasimon, during which Oidipous and the first Messenger both remain on stage.]

CHORUS

If I am a prophet indeed   *Strophe A*
and knowing in judgment,
this will happen to you,
by Olympus, oh Cithaeron:
tomorrow's full moon will exalt you   1090
as Oidipous' compatriot
and nurse and mother, and we
shall honor you in dance
for rendering such service
to my king.[117] Oh Phoibos,   1095
you to whom we cry aloud,
may this prove pleasing to you!

Who bore you, my child,   *Antistrophe A*
which of the long-lived nymphs,
consorting with your father,   1100
mountain-roving Pan?[118]

---

116 Like Oidipous, the months are "children" of Fortune, since they bring various events—for better or worse—as the moon waxes and wanes. The passage of time, as measured by the months he has lived, has "marked him out" at different times as "small and great" both literally (as a newborn and an adult) and figuratively (as a humiliated infant and a great king).

117 I.e. Cithaeron, the putative location of Oidipous' conception and birth, will be honored by an all-night festival. Such events were not uncommon (compare *Ant.* 153, 1153) The mention of the full moon provides a thematic link with Oidipous' invocation of the months as his kin (1083), but may also allude to the fact that the dramatic festival was followed by a festival held at the full moon (called the Pandia).

118 The nymphs are not immortal, like the gods, but they do live longer than human beings. They are often found in the company of Pan, a nature-god with a goat's feet and horns who lives in caves.

Or was it some bedmate of Loxias,
who loves all the upland pastures?[119]
Or was it the lord of Cyllene,
or the Bacchic god who dwells   1105
up on the mountain-peaks,
who received you as a lucky find
from one of the glancing-eyed Nymphs
with whom he so often plays?[120]

[Enter Shepherd, along the entry-ramp leading from the countryside.]

OIDIPOUS
If I must make a calculation, elders, though   1110
I've never dealt with him I think I see the herdsman
we have sought so long. This man here matches him
in his old age, which measures just as long for both;
besides, I recognize those leading him as slaves
of my own house. But you're no doubt ahead of me   1115
in knowledge, since you've seen the herdsman in the past.

CHORUS
Know well I recognize him; he was one of Laios'
men, and for a herdsman, trusty as the next.

OIDIPOUS
I ask you first, Corinthian foreigner, is this
the fellow that you meant?

MESSENGER 1
                                    The very one you see.   1120

OIDIPOUS *[to the Shepherd, whose eyes are downcast]*
You there, old man, look here and speak in answer to
the questions that I ask. Were you once Laios' slave?

SHEPHERD
Yes, I was his—not bought, but nurtured in his house.

OIDIPOUS
In what work were you occupied, or way of life?

---

119 The word translated 'pasture' (*agronomos*) echoes a title of Apollo
     (= Loxias), who is often found in the countryside and serves as a
     shepherd in several myths.
120 The lord of Cyllene, a mountain in Arcadia (see Map 1), is the god
     Hermes, who is also the god of herdsmen. Dionysos (or Bacchus) is
     another nature-god linked with mountains and nymphs.

SHEPHERD

Most of my life I've followed after flocks of sheep.   1125

OIDIPOUS

And in what region did you mostly tend your herds?

SHEPHERD

There was Cithaeron, and the lands nearby as well.

OIDIPOUS [pointing to the Corinthian messenger]

And do you know this man from meeting him round there?

SHEPHERD

What was he doing? Who's the man you're speaking of?

OIDIPOUS

This one here. Have you ever dealt with him at all?   1130

SHEPHERD

Not so that I could say at once from memory.

MESSENGER 1

That's not surprising, master. But I'll help him, though
he doesn't know me, to remember clear and true.
I'm sure he really knows that when we grazed around
Cithaeron, he with his two flocks and I with one,[121]   1135

* * * * * * * * *

I kept him company for three whole periods
of time, each six months long, from spring to Arktouros;[122]
in winter I would drive my sheep back to their barns,
and he his flocks to Laios' homesteads. Come, did any
of this happen as I say it did, or not?   1140

SHEPHERD

You speak the truth, although that time is long ago.

MESSENGER 1

Come on then, tell us: at that time, you know you gave
a child to me, to raise and nurture as my own?

SHEPHERD

What if I did? Why are you asking me all this?

MESSENGER 1

This is the man, my friend, who was that infant then.   1145

---

121 Many editors believe a line is missing here, since the Greek makes
     imperfect sense as it stands.
122 Arktouros is the brightest star in the constellation Boötes (the plowman).
     It appeared in classical Greece in mid-September.

SHEPHERD

To hell with you! Won't you be silent once for all?

OIDIPOUS

No! Don't chastise this man, old fellow; it's your words
that need chastisement rather than what he has said.

SHEPHERD

In what way, best of masters, have I been at fault?

OIDIPOUS

Not speaking of the child that this man asks about.   1150

SHEPHERD

Because he talks in ignorance and wastes his pains.

OIDIPOUS

If you won't speak to please me, you will speak in tears.

SHEPHERD

In god's name do not torture me. I'm an old man!

OIDIPOUS

Someone twist back his arms, as fast as possible![123]

SHEPHERD

What for, unhappy man? Desiring to learn what?   1155

OIDIPOUS

Did you give this man here the child of which he asks?

SHEPHERD

I did; if only I had perished on that day!

OIDIPOUS

You'll come to that if you don't give a just reply.

SHEPHERD

I'm much more certainly destroyed if I do tell.

OIDIPOUS

This man is bent on spinning out delays, it seems.   1160

SHEPHERD

No! I already said that I gave him the child.

OIDIPOUS

Where did you get it? From your house, or someone else?

SHEPHERD

Not my own child! I took it in from somebody.

---

123 This is a prelude to flogging or torture (see further Essay, p. 108).

OIDIPOUS

From which among these citizens, and from what house?

SHEPHERD

No, by the gods! No, master! Don't ask any more!   1165

OIDIPOUS

You are destroyed if I must ask you this again.

SHEPHERD

Well then, it was in Laios' house the child was born.

OIDIPOUS

A slave? Or was the infant kin to him by birth?

SHEPHERD

Alas, I'm just about to say the awful truth!

OIDIPOUS

And I to hear it; nonetheless it must be heard.   1170

SHEPHERD

All right: the child was called his own; but she who is
inside, your wife, could best tell you the truth of this.[124]

OIDIPOUS

Was she the one who gave him to you?

SHEPHERD

Yes, my lord.[125]

OIDIPOUS

What was her purpose?

SHEPHERD

That I do away with him.

OIDIPOUS

Her own child, wretch?

SHEPHERD

She dreaded evil prophecies.   1175

---

124 The word order reflects the original, in which the shepherd seems
uncertain how to refer to Jokasta, of whose true relationship to Oidipous
he is now aware. "Inside" locates her in the definitive feminine sphere of
the house, but is also somewhat ominous in light of 1071-2.

125 The division of lines between speakers marks here, as often, a heighten-
ing of tension (see further Essay, p. 125).

OIDIPOUS
What kind?

SHEPHERD
They said he'd kill the one who fathered him.

OIDIPOUS
Then why did you instead leave him with this old man?

SHEPHERD
From pity, master, thinking he would take him to
another land, where he was from; and yet he saved
him for the greatest evils; for if you are who   1180
he says, know this: ill-destined was your birth.

OIDIPOUS
Ah! Ah! It has all come out clear and true! Oh light,
may this be my last sight of you,[126] I who am now
revealed as born from those I should not, intimate
with those I should not, killing those whom I should not.   1185

*[Exeunt, Oidipous into the palace, Corinthian Messenger and Shepherd to
the countryside. The chorus dance and sing the fourth stasimon.]*

CHORUS
Ah, generations of mortals,   *Strophe A*
how I count your lives
as equal to nothingness![127]
For who, what man gains more of happiness
than just enough to think he's so,   1190
then sink like the setting sun?
Taking your divine lot,
yours, as my exemplar,
yours, poor wretched Oidipous,
I count no mortal thing as blessed.[128]   1195

---

126 This sounds like a warning of suicide, since in ancient Greek people
    often say farewell to the daylight when they are heading towards certain
    death (e.g. *Ant.* 806-10, 879-81). Oidipous' demand for a sword (1255-6)
    raises similar expectations (cf. *Ant.* 1232-9).

127 This could mean that human life is intrinsically worthless, or that
    the happiness of a human life cannot be judged until after one is
    death—a frequent sentiment in Greek texts (see e.g. the last lines
    of this play).

128 'Divine lot' translates *daimōn*, a word I have elsewhere translated as
    'divinity.' It refers loosely to all kinds of divine forces, including, as here,
    the divinely sent destiny that shapes a person's life.

You shot your arrow beyond the limit,[129]   *Antistrophe A*
winning power over a prosperity
not blessed with happiness in every way;
You destroyed—oh Zeus!—
the hook-taloned maiden, singer of oracles,   1200
and stood up as a wall of safety
against death for my land;
since then you have been called my king
and been honored most greatly
as ruler of great Thebes   1205

But now who is more miserable to hear of?   *Strophe B*
Who is at home with greater pains, or more savage
doom, his life turned upside-down?
Ah, famous royal Oidipous,
for whom the same great harbor sufficed   1210
both for the child and for the father
to fall into as bridegroom,[130] how,
oh how could the furrows plowed by your father,
endure you so long in silence?

All-seeing time has found you out against your
    will;[131]   *Antistrophe B*
it long ago passed judgment on the non-marriage   1216
marriage, which made begetter and begotten one.
Ah, child, oh child of Laios! If only,
if only I had never seen you![132]
How I lament for you above all others,   1220

---

129 This image refers to Oidipous' supreme, almost superhuman success
    in outwitting the Sphinx. At the same time, the idea of going beyond a
    boundary or limitation is an ominous one (cf. 124, 873-8).
130 The "harbor" is Jokasta's womb (cf. 421-3).
131 Time is often personified and invested with divine omniscience and
    justice (compare 614, *OC* 1453-5). Oidipous did, of course, desire to
    find out the truth about himself. But the discovery was "against his
    will" in the sense that no one could actually want to learn such facts
    about himself.
132 This is not simply an expression of selfishness on the part of the chorus,
    who remain devoted to Oidipous. Rather, it expresses the wish that
    none of this should ever have happened, and in particular, that Laios'
    child should never have survived to stand before them in the person
    of Oidipous. Similarly 1348.

pouring cries forth from my mouth!
To tell it straight, it was from you that I drew breath,
from you I closed my eyes in sleep.[133]

[The Second Messenger enters from the palace and addresses the chorus.]

MESSENGER 2

Oh you always most greatly honored in this land,
what deeds you'll hear about, what sights you'll see, what
  sorrow
you will shoulder—if you still pay due attention   1225
to the house of Labdakos, as kinsmen should. [134]
The Istros or the Phasis, [135] so I think, could not
wash clean this dwelling-place, such evils it conceals,
and some of them will shortly be revealed to light—
things willed, not done against the will. Disasters that   1230
are shown to be self-chosen bring the greatest pain.[136]

CHORUS

What we already knew about was fully burdened
with lament. What do you have to add to that?

MESSENGER 2

The quickest thing to speak and learn about is death:
she's dead, Jokasta, our own royal, godlike queen.[137]   1235

---

133 The interpretation of these lines is controversial. The most likely
    meaning is: you have brought me both life (by killing the Sphinx)
    and the "sleep" of death (i.e. the plague, or the metaphorical death of
    despair). Alternatively, the whole sentence might mean simply "you
    were everything to me."

134 The chorus are Oidipous' kinsmen since, as noblemen, they too are
    descended from the Kadmeian stock to which the royal house belongs.

135 The Istros and Phasis are two great rivers at the edges of the Greek
    world. The Istros in Northern Europe is the modern Danube. The
    Phasis lies beyond the Black Sea and was viewed as the boundary
    between Europe and Asia.

136 In the chorus's opinion, self-inflicted suffering is the most painful because
    it cannot be blamed on an external cause. Other characters, such as
    Oidipous himself, would not necessarily agree with this sentiment.

137 Because Jokasta's name is delayed, for a split second the chorus and
    audience may think that it is Oidipous who is dead, as the wording of
    his last exit led us to expect (see n. on 1183). "Godlike" is a Homeric
    epithet of kings, but has more ominous overtones in view of this family's
    special relationship to the gods (Essay, p. 94).

CHORUS
Alas, poor wretched one! What was responsible?

MESSENGER 2
She did it to herself. The deed's most grievous part
is absent, since the vision of it is not here.
But still, as far as memory can report, you shall
discover what she suffered—miserable one.   1240
    When she had passed inside the palace entry-way
frantic with passionate grief, she rushed straight to her bridal
bed, tearing her hair with fingers of both hands.
Once in her room, she slammed the doors shut and called out
to Laios, now long since a corpse, reminding him   1245
about the seed he sowed so long ago, which brought
him death and left herself, who bore that child, for his
own son to father misbegotten children on.
She mourned the bed where she, unhappy one, gave birth
twice over: husband from her husband, children from   1250
her child. And then she perished, but I don't know how,
for Oidipous struck his way in there, screaming; this
kept us from seeing out her evil to the end;[138]
so it was him we stared at as he roamed the house.
He ranged about, imploring us to furnish him   1255
a sword and tell him where to find his non-wife wife,
the twice-plowed field that bore his children and himself.
And in his frenzy some divine power pointed out
the way—for it was none of us, the men nearby.
He gave an awful cry, then leaped against the double   1260
doors, as if he had a guide, bent both the panels
inward from their frame, and fell into the room.
We saw the woman in there dangling, with her neck
entangled in the twisted noose from which she swung.
On seeing her, the poor man bellowed awfully   1265
and loosed the knot that held her dangling. When she lay,

---

138 Since Jokasta has locked her bedroom doors from the inside, the
    Messenger must mean that he and the other attendants were distracted
    by Oidipous' entrance into the house from listening further to Jokasta
    or trying to enter the chamber and find out what was happening. But
    his language suggests rather that of the theatrical spectator who is
    prevented from viewing a performance to the end.

poor wretch, upon the ground, next came an awful sight.
He tore off from her dress the pair of gold-wrought pins
that kept it in due order,[139] raised them up and struck
them in his eyeballs in their sockets, crying out   1270
that they should never see him or the evils he
had suffered and had done, but should in future look
in darkness on the people he should not have seen,
and fail to recognize those he'd desired to find.
While chanting things like this, he lifted up the pins   1275
and gouged his eyes with them, not once but many times.[140]
The bleeding eye-balls drenched his cheeks, not just emitting
slowly oozing drops of blood, but drenching him
with the black downpour of a storm of bloody hail.
Such are the evils that have broken forth from two,   1280
not one: the mingled evils of a man and wife.
Their past prosperity from long ago was justly
so-called; but now, on this day, there is no groaning
cry, no doom, disgrace or death, no evil thing
that can be named, with which they are not intimate.[141]   1285

CHORUS

Poor wretch—and have his evils slackened off by now?

MESSENGER 2

He screams for someone to throw wide the doors and show
to all the Kadmeians his father's killer and
his mother's... I can't utter his unholy words;
he means to throw himself forth from the land, and not   1290
stay in this house, accursed as he has cursed himself.[142]
But he needs someone to support and guide him, since
the sickness that afflicts him is too great to bear.
He will display this to your eyes as well; for see,
the gates are opening; soon you will gaze upon   1295
a sight of such a kind that even one who felt

---

139 A woman's clothing was secured on both shoulders with brooches,
   similar in construction to modern safety-pins, but much larger.
140 The verb "chanting" conveys both repetition and the power of a curse
   or ritual act (compare *Ant.* 658, 1304-5).
141 Compare the list of disasters that have stricken the family at *Ant.* 1-6.
142 The curse that Oidipous inadvertently placed on himself will continue
   to contaminate his family and house if he remains there (compare
   236-42).

abhorrence for the man would surely pity him.[143]

[Oidipous enters from the palace, with a new mask showing his blindness. After fourteen lines of anapests (1298-1311) and a single trimeter (1312) he and the chorus participate in a kommos (lyric dialogue) which includes both lyric and iambic lines.]

CHORUS

> *Oh suffering awful for humankind*
> *to see, most awful of all that I've ever*
> *encountered! What mad frenzy, wretch,*   1300
> *came over you? What divinity has*
> *leapt further than furthest against you in your*
> *divinely sent and wretched destiny?*
> *Woe, woe, unhappy one! I can't even*
> *look at you, though there are many things I*   1305
> *want to ask, to discover, to gaze at—*
> *such is the shuddering you provoke in me.*[144]

OIDIPOUS

> *Aiai! Aiai! Unhappy me!*
> *Where on earth am I carried to, wretch that I am?*[145]
> *Where does my voice rush fluttering off to?*   1310
> *Ah, divinity, where have you leapt to?*[146]

CHORUS

To somewhere awful, neither heard nor looked upon.

OIDIPOUS

> Ah, my cloud of darkness   *Strophe A*
> horrific, overwhelming, unspeakable,   1315
> invincible, wafted by an evil wind!
> Alas!

---

143 This could mean either that even an enemy who hated Oidipous would pity him, or that he would be pitied even by someone appalled by his deeds and the sight he presents.

144 For the chorus' mingled reaction of fascination and horror compare *OC* 510-48.

145 Oidipous' use of the passive indicates his helplessness as a blind man. But it also suggests the other wanderings, metaphorical and literal, of a life that has been directed by forces of which he was unaware.

146 Fate or misfortune is often imagined as "leaping" on the head of its victims (compare 263, 1300-1302, *Ant.* 1344-7). In this case, however, Oidipous imagines his fate as having leapt not upon his head, but into a distant (i.e. extreme and alien) location.

Alas once more! How they have pierced me, both at once,
the stinging of these goads and memory of my evils![147]

CHORUS

It's no surprise that in such great disasters you   1320
should sorrow doubly, cry out doubly at your evils.

OIDIPOUS

Ah friend!   *Antistrophe A*
You are my steadfast attendant! For you
still stay to tend me, blind as I am!
Alas, alas!   1325
I am not unaware of you; although I am
in darkness, I still clearly recognize your voice.

CHORUS

You who have done these awful deeds, how could you bear
to quench your vision thus? What god incited you?

OIDIPOUS

It was Apollo, my friends, Apollo   *Strophe B*
who fulfilled my evil, these my evil sufferings.[148]   1331
But the murderous hand that struck me
was no one's but my own,
wretch that I am!
Why should I see, when there   1335
was nothing sweet for me to see if I had sight?

CHORUS

That's how it was, just as you say.

OIDIPOUS

What sight for me to see
could be cherished?
What address could be heard   1340
with pleasure, friends?
Lead me from this place
as fast as possible,

---

147 "Stinging" refers to the sting of the gadfly, which was so painful
that it was thought to cause madness. The "goads" are the two pins
with which Oidipous pierced his eyes, but the word also recalls the
two-pronged goad with which Laios struck him (809), and his parents'
"two-pronged" curse (417-19).

148 On the meaning of this passage see Essay, pp. 128-9.

lead me away, friends, utterly lost,
most utterly accursed,   1345
and also to the gods
most utterly hateful of mortals!

CHORUS
Oh how I wish I'd never known you, equally
as wretched in your mind as in your circumstances.

OIDIPOUS
May the wanderer perish, whoever he was,   *Antistrophe B*
who took from my feet the savage shackles,   1351
rescued me from death
and saved me—
doing me no favor;
for if I'd died then I'd not have   1355
brought all this grief to both my dear ones and myself.

CHORUS
I too would have wished this to be so.

OIDIPOUS
Then I'd not have come here
as my father's murderer,
and mortals would not call me   1360
bridegroom of her who bore me.
As it is, I'm god-forsaken,
child of impiety, sharing fatherhood
with him who gave me birth,
wretch that I am!   1365
If any evil outranks evil,
that is the allotment of Oidipous.

CHORUS
I don't know how to say you planned this well; you would
do better to exist no longer than live blind.

OIDIPOUS
Don't try to tell me that what I have done was not
done for the best! Don't give me any more advice!   1370
If I had sight, I don't know with what eyes I could
have looked upon my father when I went to Hades,
and my poor wretched mother; I've done deeds to both
of them so dire that hanging is too good for me.
Or did my children—born as they were born—provide   1375

a vision that I might desire to gaze upon?
No, never! Never with these eyes of mine at least.
No, nor the town, its walls, its images
and temples of divinities, which I, most finely
nurtured of all men in Thebes, I wretched one,   1380
deprived myself of, when I did myself proclaim
that all should thrust out the irreverent man, the one
revealed by gods to be impure and Laios' kin.
After declaring such a stain upon myself
was I to look with straight eyes at these people here?[148]   1385
No! Rather, if there was some way to block the flow
of hearing through my ears, I would not have held back
from closing off my miserable body in
this way as well, to make me deaf as well as blind—
it's sweet for thought to dwell apart from evil things.   1390
    Ah why, Cithaeron, did you take me in? Oh why
did you not kill me straight away, so that I never
could display my origins to human kind?
Oh Polybos, and Corinth, so-called fatherland
of long ago, you nursed me as a thing of beauty   1395
festering with evil underneath the skin;
now I'm found out as evil and of evil birth.
Oh you three paths, you hidden glade, you woods, you narrow
place where three roads meet, who drank in at my hands
the blood that flows in my own veins, my father's blood,   1400
do you remember still what deeds I did there in
your presence, and what further actions I performed
when I came here? Oh marriage, marriage, you both gave
me birth, and after I was born from you again
raised up my seed, displaying to the world fathers   1405
as brothers, children shedding kindred blood, brides as
both wives and mothers, all the utterly disgraceful
deeds that can occur among the human race.
    But it's not fine to speak of things not fine to do.

---

149 To look someone in the eye is a sign of frankness, honesty, and/or a
     sound mind, suggesting that one has nothing to be ashamed of (cf. 528,
     523-5). To do so when one is disgraced is considered an affront to the
     person in question. In this case, of course, Oidipous is also referring to
     his inability to look at anyone at all, owing to his blindness (cf. 419),
     which itself expresses the intensity of his sense of shame.

So by the gods, hide me as fast as possible   1410
outside this land, or murder me, or throw me in
the sea, where you may never look on me again.
Come, don't disdain to touch a miserable man;
let me persuade you, do not dread me; for my evils
can't be borne by any mortal but myself.[150]   1415

CHORUS

Just when you need him for the deeds and plans that you
are begging for, here's Kreon; he's the only person left
to take your place as guardian of this land.

OIDIPOUS

Alas, how shall I speak to him? What cause has he
to trust me in all justice? I have been found out   1420
as evil to him in the past in every way.

[Enter Kreon along the entry ramp leading from the city.]

KREON

I have not come here, Oidipous, to laugh at you,
nor to reproach you with the evils of the past.

[He addresses the chorus and attendants.]

You, even if you've lost all sense of shame before
mere mortal creatures, then at least respect the flame   1425
that feeds all things, lord Helios, and don't display
uncovered such a curse as this, which neither earth
nor sacred rain nor light is willing to take in.[151]
Come now, take him from here, as fast as possible,
inside the house; for reverence requires that only   1430
kindred see and hear the evils of their kin.

---

150 Religious pollution is normally infectious, affecting the polluted
person's immediate relatives most directly (cf. 1430-31), but also making
it dangerous for others to approach and especially to touch him or her
(cf. *OC* 1132-6). At this moment, however, Oidipous feels so uniquely
contaminated that his pollution can be transmitted to no one else, nor
can anyone be expected to share any part of his burden of suffering.

151 Kreon invokes all the constituent elements of the universe: earth, "light"
or air, fire, and water (symbolized by rain). This signifies the rejection
of Oidipous by the whole physical world, as well as the land of Thebes
(see further Essay, p. 131).

OIDIPOUS

It's not what I expected, that you come here, best
of men, to me the evilest; so by the gods
let me persuade you—for your own sake, not for mine.

KREON

What's this request you beg for so insistently?   1435

OIDIPOUS

Throw me, as fast as possible, out of this land,
somewhere no mortal can address or look on me.

KREON

I would have done so—know this well—if I did not
desire to learn first from the god what must be done.

OIDIPOUS

His voice said clearly and in full that I, the father-   1440
killer, the irreverent one, should be destroyed.

KREON

That's what was said; yet where we stand now in our need
it's better that we learn for certain what to do.

OIDIPOUS

You will inquire for such a miserable man?

KREON

I will; perhaps this time you too may trust the god.   1445

OIDIPOUS

I will; but it is you I now enjoin and urge:
arrange what burial you want for her within
the house; it's right that you fulfill this for your kin.[152]
But as for me, let this my fathers' town not be
deemed worthy to obtain me as a resident   1450
while I'm alive; but let me dwell up in the mountains
in my own place, called Cithairon, which my mother
and my father, while they were still living, chose
as my appointed place of burial, so that my death
may come from those attempting to destroy me then.
Yet I know this: no sickness and no other cause   1455
could kill me; I would never have been saved from dying

---

152 Oidipous avoids mentioning his mother-wife by name (contrast 950).
   After the announcement of her death (1235), Jokasta's name is not
   spoken again.

then, except to meet some awful evil end.[153]

    But let my destiny go where it will; as for
my children, though, do not preoccupy yourself,
Kreon, about the boys; they're men, so they will never   1460
lack for livelihood wherever they may be;
but my two piteous and miserable girls,
whose food was always set at my own table, so
that they were never parted from this man, but always
shared, the two of them, in what I touched—with these   1465
two do concern yourself; above all, let me touch
them with my hands and shed tears for our evil lot.[154]
Come, my lord![155]
Come, noble in your birth! If my hands held them I
would think I had them as I did when I could see.   1470

*[Enter Antigone and Ismene from within the house, weeping and led
by an attendant.[156]]*

What is that?
Oh gods, can it be true? Can I be hearing them,
my dear ones, streaming tears? Has Kreon pitied me
and sent to me my offspring, these two dearest ones?
Am I right?   1475

KREON

You're right. I brought about this visit, knowing you
would still delight in them as you have done so long.

---

153 Oidipous senses that even if he is once more abandoned on Cithaeron,
as his parents wished, he will once again be saved from a normal death,
because his story so far has been so remarkable. In *Oidipous at Colonus*
Sophocles dramatized his extraordinary death.

154 In classical Athens, young girls would not dine with their father. The
description reflects a conception of the heroic age as freer in such
matters. But it also suggests a special intensity in Oidipous' relationship
to his daughters (cf. Essay, p. 130).

155 Oidipous' iambic trimeters are punctuated three times (1468, 1471,
1475) by short exclamatory phrases, in a rare technique expressive
of high emotion.

156 The girls' ages are not specified, but they are too young to understand
rational advice from their father (1511). The exact moment of their
entrance is uncertain. Some editors think they enter with Kreon and
are silent until now. Alternatively, Kreon may have sent an attendant
for them earlier.

OIDIPOUS

May fortune favor you! May some divinity
perchance protect you better than myself, for this,
their road to me. Where are you, children? Come to me!   1480
Come to your brother's hands, which did a favor to
the eyes, once shining, of the father who begot
you both, by making them see thus—the father now
revealed as having sown you, children, in the place
where he was sown, unseeing and unquestioning.   1485
I weep for you two also—since I lack the strength
to look at you—my mind upon the bitter life
that still remains for you to live at human hands.
What gatherings of townsfolk will you now attend,
what public festivals, without returning home   1490
in tears, instead of gazing at the spectacle?[157]
And when you reach the proper age for marriage, who
will be the one, my children? Who will run the risk
of taking on the kind of insults that will cling
disastrously to both your parents and yourselves?   1495
What evil is not here? Your father murdered his
own father; plowed the one who bore him, in the place
where he himself was sown, and thus in that same place
from which he had his birth begot you equally.
Insulted for all this, who then will marry you?   1500
The man does not exist, my children; clearly you
must waste away in barren, childless spinsterhood.
    Son of Menoikeus, you're the only father left
to these two girls, since both of us who gave them birth
have perished; father, don't stand by and watch them, your   1505
own kinsfolk, wandering as vagrant beggars without
husbands; do not make their evils equal mine.
Take pity on them, seeing them bereft so young
of everything except what you may offer them.

---

157 Even in classical Athens, where women were barred from participation
in political life, they might attend certain public religious festivals,
some of which included such "spectacles" as processions, and indeed
the drama itself (Introduction, pp. 7-8). Such festivals were an integral
part of the life of the city-state and also the family, which would be
disgraced if its members were excluded from participating.

Touch me, consenting, with your hand, oh noble one.[158]   1510
    For you two, children, if you understood, I would
have much advice; but as it is, make this your prayer:
to live where opportunity permits, and meet
a better life than me, the father of your birth.

[The remainder of the play is in trochaic tetrameters, an unusual meter
for tragedy, with slightly longer lines than iambic trimeters; they are
translated here with eight iambic beats.]

KREON
You have gone far enough in shedding tears; now go
    inside the house.   1515
OIDIPOUS
Though it's not sweet, I must obey.[159]
KREON
                    What's opportune is always fine.
OIDIPOUS
Then do you know what terms I'll go on?
KREON
                    Speak, then I shall hear and know.
OIDIPOUS
Send me forth homeless from this land.
KREON
                    You ask what is the god's to give.
OIDIPOUS
I've come to be most hateful to the gods.
KREON
                    Then you'll soon get your wish.
OIDIPOUS
Is that a "yes"?
KREON
              I do not like to say in vain what I don't think.[160]   1520

---

158 The blind Oidipous cannot see if Kreon is nodding in assent (the literal
    meaning of the verb), so he asks for a touch of the hand instead. His
    request also suggest the clasping of right hands as a token of agreement
    between two men. A touch of the hand might also signify affection
    (compare 1466-7).
159 The word "obey" is in Greek the same as "be persuaded" (compare
    650, 1064).
160 This could imply either "Yes" or "No" in answer to Oidipous' question.

OIDIPOUS

Then lead me now away from here.

KREON:

Go now, but let your children go.

OIDIPOUS

No, don't take them away from me!

KREON

Don't wish for power in everything;
the power that once was yours did not attend you through the
course of life.

*[Exeunt Oidipous into the palace, led by attendants, the other characters
along the entry ramp leading to the city. The chorus conclude the play
with a final reflection addressed to each other,[161] then exeunt in the
direction of the city.]*

CHORUS

Oh you who make your home in Thebes, our fatherland, see
Oidipous!
Behold the overwhelming wave of awful circumstances he   1525
has entered, he who knew the famous riddles and who was a
man
most powerful, whose fortune everyone among the citizens
looked on with envy. Therefore one should never say a mortal
man
is prosperous while he still waits to look upon his final day,
until he passes life's last limit having suffered no distress.   1530

---

161 For various technical reasons, many scholars believe this final choral
tag is spurious.

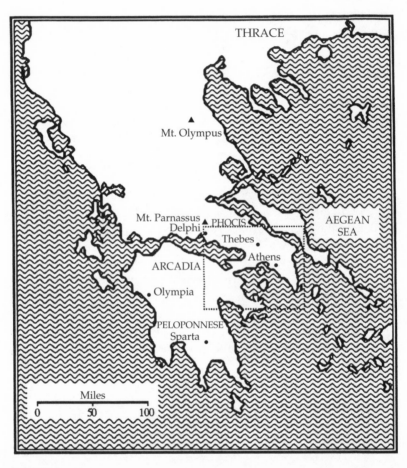

MAP 1
MAINLAND GREECE

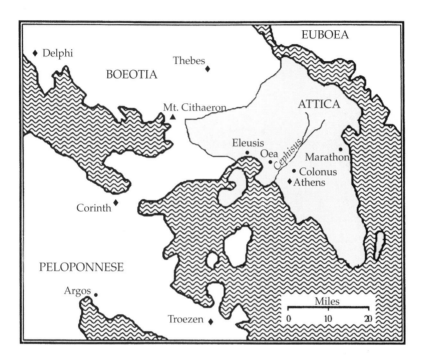

MAP 2
ATTICA AND ENVIRONS

King Oidipous: Essay

King Oidipous tells the story of a remarkably intelligent investigator uncovering the identity of a mysterious criminal. As such, it has much in common with the contemporary genre of the murder mystery, in which a detective discovers a killer's identity and reveals it at the climax to an awestruck audience, usually including the dead person's heirs and next of kin. What sets its plot structure apart from the modern genre, however, is that in *King Oidipous* the detective, the killer, the stunned audience, the heir and the next of kin are all one person: Oidipous himself. Furthermore, the play resounds with the language of the Athenian democratic courts. If we view the play as an antecedent of the courtroom drama, Oidipous is not only the perpetrator who is "tried" and condemned, but the lawyer on both sides of the case, the jury, and a key witness for both defense and prosecution. This fusion of roles that are normally distinct, in the investigations of life as well as those of fiction, is in part what allows this story to serve as the vehicle of a profound exploration of questions of human knowledge, human nature, and the mysteries of identity.

Sophocles opens most of his surviving plays (including both *Antigone* and *Oidipous at Colonus*) with an intimate encounter among just two or three characters. But he chose to begin *King Oidipous* with a public scene in which the king emerges from the palace to address a crowd of suppliant citizens in desperate need. The presence of children especially enhances the pathos of the city's plight, evoking the way in which Athenian defendants brought their children into court to arouse the sympathy of the jury. This helpless crowd conveys a picture of Oidipous, by contrast, as a king at the pinnacle of his power and status, a great man, a public benefactor, and a benevolent ruler. In the first words of the play he addresses the whole group as his "children," suggesting that all the Thebans are in a child-like, dependent relationship to him (1; cf. 58, 143). This paternal concern is one of his many admirable qualities as a king, which also include compassion (58-67), openness (cf. 93), and vigorous action on his people's behalf. The unusually full prologue contains an exceptional amount of action, which conveys an impression of swift, decisive resourcefulness. Thus Oidipous, after careful forethought, has already sent Kreon, his brother-in-law, to consult the oracle at Delphi, and is impatient that this action has not already borne fruit (66-75). We will see the same foresight—and impatience—in him again later (284-9). The effectiveness of these qualities is endorsed by the track record that brought him the kingship, which he received as a reward for solving the riddle of the Sphinx (Introduction, p. 18). This success depended on his most salient trait—his superior intelligence. His characteristic "weapon" is the "spear of thought" (170), which he wields in an energetic and practical fashion.

The priest emphasizes that Oidipous' victory over the Sphinx was achieved through divine assistance as well as human experience and planning (34-43). He also underlines Oidipous' extraordinary power (14), rather startlingly refers to the altar as "your altar" (15), without mentioning the god Apollo to whom it is dedicated, and calls him the city's "savior" (48; cf. 443), which is an official title of Zeus himself and may also be used of other gods, such as Apollo (cf. 150). In response Oidipous promises to fight as their "ally" (135, 244)—another word often used in invoking the help of the gods. And when he re-emerges from the palace after the parodos, it is as if he were answering the chorus' prayer (216). Other verbal parallels also equate him subtly with the gods (compare 14 with 903, 150 with 397, 189 with 42 and 218, 199 with 237, 259 and 383 with 905, 441 with 872). And he himself will speculate, as the climax of the play approaches, that he is in some sense of divine birth (1080-83).

Indeed, Oidipous' status in relation to his people approaches so closely to that of a divine savior that the priest needs to emphasize that they do not view him as a god, but only as "the first of men" (31-4). This distinguishes him from the kind of objectionable ruler who does expect his subjects to treat him like a god—something that offends both democratic Athenians and the gods themselves. Nonetheless, the audience might well wonder both whether the Thebans rely on this one man to excess, and whether his eminence is such that he can only fall from it, simply because, in a commonly expressed Greek view, great human success cannot last forever (cf. e.g. *Ant.* 612-4. Sophocles dramatizes this view later in the play by having the chorus sing an ode that equates Oidipous with the gods right before his downfall (1086-1109; cf. below, p.124). That downfall results from Oidipous' acquisition of self-knowledge, of a kind embodied in the famous dictum "know yourself." This injunction, over which Apollo presides, very often means understanding that one is merely mortal, and not a god.

The present crisis for which Oidipous' aid is sought is a devastating plague. Whether or not this description was inspired by the plague at Athens (Introduction, p. 16), it makes complete sense in mythic/symbolic terms. The Theban plague has been caused by a "pollution" (95-8), an invisible and infectious religious taint (Introduction, p. 000). The extremity of this particular pollution arises from the extraordinary violations of the natural order represented by Oidipous' unwitting acts of incest and parricide. The plague is accompanied by corresponding perversions of fertility and reproduction among humans, animals and crops (see 25-30 with note; also 171-3). The interconnection between these various natural processes is expressed through the pervasive use of agricultural imagery for human reproduction in general, and Oidipous' incestuous family in particular (e.g. 1211-13, 1244-8, 1257, 1403-5, 1496-9). While this royal house, with its confusion of reproductive roles, is rich in children, the land it rules is barren and diseased (compare 1403-5 with 269-71). The rejection of "normal" reproductive familial life, and thus its own extinction, is the only possible "solution" for this particular family, as can be seen in Sophocles' play *Antigone*, where the heroine—Oidipous' incestuous daughter—rejects marriage and reproduction in favor of loyalty to her dead father's family (*Ant.* 904-14; cf. also *OT* 1492-1502).

As an admirable king, Oidipous identifies strongly with the city of Thebes as a whole (60-64, 93-4). Since he himself will emerge as the epicenter of the plague, there is heavy irony in his compassionate claim to be the most "sick" of all the citizens (60-64). This psychological "sickness," or suffering on behalf of his people's pain, is transformed by the end of the play into the "sickness" of unutterable personal anguish (1293; cf. 1061), which finds physical expression in Oidipous' self-blinding. His sorrow for the city turns out to be indeed sorrow about his own life (93-4). The city in question is, of course, Thebes. But Thebes, as often in tragedy, may also be viewed as a kind of "anti-Athens," allowing the Athenian audience to look at themselves in the mirror of myth without overtly attaching such unsavory events to their own city (Introduction, p. 16). And Oidipous in particular is often seen as emblematic of Athens, since he embodies many aspects of the Athenian self-image at this period, such as vigor, intelligence, decisiveness, versatility, patriotism, self-confidence and a spirit of inquiry. On the negative side, Athens enjoyed an autocratic rule over its subject-allies which was viewed by many, according to the contemporary historian Thucydides, as a form of "tyranny" (1.122, 1.124., 2.63, 3.37, 6.85). The legalistic tone of the drama also reflects the language of the courtroom, a central and defining aspect of Athenian democratic culture. One influential interpretation of the play has therefore seen it as a commentary on the strengths and limitations of Athens at the height of its power (Knox 1998).

Some readers have seen a more specific and personal analogy between Oidipous and Pericles, the Athenian general and statesman who helped elevate Athens to its political and artistic pre-eminence (see esp. Ehrenberg 1954). Like Pericles, at least in Thucydides' account, Oidipous is an admirable and remarkable leader. And even though Athens was a democracy, Pericles' rule, like that of Oidipous over Thebes, combined autocratic and democratic elements (cf. below, pp. 107-9). His power derived from his repeated election to the post of general, yet in practice, according to Thucydides, his was the rule of a single man (2.65.9). The need to drive out a polluting presence, in the form of an aristocratic leader, may have reminded Athenians of a demand by the Spartans for expulsion of Pericles' family in order to expiate an ancestral murder (Thuc. 1.126-7). (The word translated "purge" at 401 particularly evokes this expulsion.) Moreover, if the scholars who date this play after the beginning of the Peloponnesian war are correct, it was produced shortly after Pericles' death in the plague, at the height of his own and Athens' power. Like Oidipous, he was a great and patriotic ruler felled by a seemingly random disaster from a world outside human understanding and control.

Whether or not we think Oidipous serves as an image of Pericles or of Sophocles' Athens, it is clear that he represents not only kingship but manhood at its apogee. Since Greek ideology views the adult male more generally as the ideal human self, he is also emblematic of that self, which is defined in large part by the exclusion of contrasted and usually inferior others: the old, the young, the female, the "barbarian" (i.e. non-Greek; cf. below, p. 107). The opening group of suppliants represents the full spectrum of age-groups within the city: youths and children are present as well as old men. The only adult male in the prime of life in this tableau is Oidipous himself. These various age groups recall the three ages of "man" in the riddle of the Sphinx. On this analogy, Oidipous is the human being at mid-day, in the prime of life, who stands upright without support, in contrast to the helpless old and young seated before him, and the aged priest, who would probably stand leaning on a staff. This role as an emblem of humanity as such will develop as the play proceeds, until Oidipous becomes an exemplar not of manly strength, but of the wretchedness of all humanity (1192-5). It also gives special point to the way he repeatedly points to himself in the third person ("this man here"), especially as an archetype of human misery (534, 814-5, 828-9, 1464). This is a common Greek idiom for referring to oneself, which may serve to add pathos or emphasise the speaker's dignity (cf. 1018). But in this play, it acquires special resonance from Oidipous' larger iconic status.

Paradoxically, however, this role is complemented by a repeated emphasis on Oidipous' uniqueness, which harks back to the heroic individualism of the Greek epic tradition. In contrast to the anonymous crowd that surrounds him, he proclaims himself "famous in all eyes, the man called Oidipous" (8). These words echo those of Homeric heroes such as Odysseus, who introduces himself to strangers with the declaration, "I am Odysseus son of Laertes, whose fame reaches up to the sky" (*Odyssey* 9.19). A modern reader might be tempted to see such pronouncements as unattractively boastful. The modern hero who, like Mohammed Ali, declares "I'm the greatest" is the exception, not the rule. But in the mouth of a Greek hero, they are simply statements of fact. Humility, modesty and self-deprecation are not characteristic virtues of the ancient Greek male. A century after Sophocles, Aristotle would declare that the most completely virtuous man is one who is fully aware of his own superiority (*Nicomachean Ethics* 4.3). Oidipous' superiority to other men is denied by no one, and is fundamental to the meaning of the play as a whole. His willingness to acknowledge it should not be construed as a shortcoming. At the same time, this pronouncement would produce an ironic effect on the original audience, to whom Oidipous' name was most famous as a token of unspeakable human suffering.

Oidipous' public pronouncement of his own name introduces another central complex of ideas: the relationship between naming and personal identity. In the world of Homeric epic, to be named sets one apart from the anonymous masses of the battlefield, and enables one to be commemorated in epic song. Yet to be named is also to be identifiable and thus at risk. Homer's Odysseus brings down disaster on his crew by annoucing his real name, after he has escaped from the murderous cyclops Polyphemos by claiming that his name is "No One" (*Odyssey* 9.502-36). In religious and magical traditions, knowledge of a person's name gives one power over him or her. Moreover Greek authors routinely attributed serious import to the real or apparent meanings of names, and played on these meanings freely, often in situations where the modern reader might find such a pun to be inappropriately frivolous. Their interest was not in the scientific discovery of etymologies or the "true" meaning of a name, so much as in the symbolic associations of even the most fanciful "derivations." In King Oidipous such puns have a further dimension, in so far as they express linguistically the riddling nature of reality, and in particular of human nature, which is so central to the play.

The various possible meanings of Oidipous' name are particularly significant to his story. To the Greek audience, the meaning of *pous* would have been obvious: it means "foot" (it is related to English words like "podiatry," "tripod," and "octopus"). The first element (*oid-*) suggests two possibilities. One is a Greek word for swelling. "Oidipous" would thus mean "swollen-foot." The shepherd will later explain the name this way. In the absence of the social identity provided by parental naming, the infant Oidipous was named "who he is" by those who rescued him, from the disfigurement of his feet (1036). The shepherd's wording here establishes an exceptionally intimate relationship between naming and identity. But *oid-* also suggests *oida,* the most common Greek verb for knowing. This verb is in turn related to a linguistic root for seeing (*wid-*, which gives us the English word "video"). The link between seeing and knowing makes intuitive sense, since when one has seen something, one presumably knows it—a connection played upon throughout the play, with its interlacing of vision and knowledge (cf. e.g. 118-19, where the word-play is evident in Greek). This derivation too is well suited to Oidipous' identity. Although his name may not in fact derive from this root (its origin is disputed), *King Oidipous* is replete with puns on the name of Oidipous as knower (cf. esp. 43 with note, 397 with note).

If we put this interpretation of the name's first element together with the second, then the name as a whole can be interpreted as "he who knows feet." On the face of it, this might seem to mean little. But the story of Oidipous, together with its treatment in this play, in fact gives feet enormous significance. First, there is the riddle of the Sphinx, which Oidipous solves precisely by understanding the significance of "feet." Then there is the recognition of the significance of his own mutilated feet, which will constitute recognition of his identity, the central "riddle" of the play. Drawing upon both possible meanings of *oid-*, Oidipous is eventually one who knows the meaning of his own swollen feet. Foot imagery keeps reappearing in powerful and sometimes unexpected ways (below, pp. 104-5, 110, 119, 122). This gives thematic resonance even to ordinary idioms such as "underfoot" (128), "at our feet" (131) and "beneath my feet" (445)—all of which have the word "foot" in the original Greek as well as in English.

The foot motif is inextricable from another central theme—that of traveling. The second element of Oidipous' name resembles a word meaning "where" (*pou*)—a meaning that is punned on most strikingly in the Corinthian messenger's three opening lines (923-5; see note), and may lie behind some of Teiresias' ominous statements (367, 413-14). On this interpretation the name would suggest that Oidipous is someone who knows—or does not know—where he is in life. The "voyage" or "path" of life is a commonplace metaphor in Greek texts, as in English, and is implied in the riddle of the Sphinx. Travel is also one of the most ancient and pervasive metaphors for intellectual inquiry, and the play is replete with such imagery (e.g. 67, 108-9). In Oidipous' case, both these images are made concrete by his travels (on foot) from Corinth to Delphi to Thebes, which he retraces intellectually to discover the truth about himself. This truth in turn can only be learned by coming to understand the prior journey, from cradle to Corinth, with which his life began. It is by making various choices along both the path of inquiry and the literal road beneath his feet that Oidipous becomes an emblem for the passage of all humanity along the path of life. In this context, even commonplace idioms of motion and location (which are far more frequent in Greek than English) gain added weight (e.g. 108, 124, 324, 367, 673-4, 685-7, 771-3, 953, 971-2, 1442, 1458, 1515). Tracking and hunting form further natural complements to these themes, linking them, for example, with the "hunting down" of the killer (e.g. 108-11, 221-2). This web of images is extended still further through imagery of light and darkness, sight and revelation—the other most prevalent set of images for intellectual discovery, complementing that of the path of discovery. Although this too is a frequent pattern of imagery in Greek culture (as in English), it is specially significant in this play, not only because of its exceptional pervasiveness, but because of the literalizing of images of sight and blindness in the persons of Teiresias and Oidipous.

Oidipous has just informed his people, in the prologue, that he has sent Kreon to consult the oracle at Delphi, when Kreon arrives back, seemingly by chance, exactly at the moment when he is needed (78-9). This is the first of a number of such "coincidences" throughout the play (compare e.g. 631, 1416-17). It is also the first of many moments where what seems to be good news or a source of consolation turns out to be the opposite. Of course it is quite common in the theater for characters to show up just when they are needed, for dramatic convenience (cf. e.g. *Ant*. 386, 1180-82). But such moments will turn out to have more sinister significance in this particular play, whose story is constructed out of a disturbing web of coincidence. The single survivor of Laios' murder, for example, will turn out to be the same man who was ordered to abandon the infant Oidipous on the mountain. And both Oidipous and his father, who might have passed their whole lives without meeting, just happen to be travelling to and from Delphi, respectively, when they encounter each other at place in the road that is too narrow for two people to pass each other. The significance of even Kreon's "chance" arrival in the prologue is clear from the fact that he brings a message from Apollo, who will turn out to lie behind many of the other coincidences in the story of Oidipous' life. Dramatic structure in this case is not simply a convenience, but replicates larger underlying narrative and mythic structures, suggesting that even life's most apparently random events may have a hidden pattern that we mortals cannot perceive.

Kreon's news provides Oidipous, in the role of "detective," with his first "witness," supplying "evidence" to which he can apply his famous intellect. Their conversation takes the form of double stichomythia (see Introduction, p. 15). This formal structure is ideally suited to the dramatic representation of "courtroom" interrogation, the construction of chains of evidence, the gradual revelation of clues, and the eventual piecing together of a puzzle. It therefore bulks unusually large in this particular play. The main plot does not consist in dramatic "action" as commonly understood, but rather in the passage from ignorance to understanding of past actions. Question and answer form, as formalized through stichomythia, is therefore thematically appropriate as well as formally convenient. Through the gradual dissemination of information it helps to create dramatic tension where there is very little action of a conventional kind. It also serves to reinforce the courtroom atmosphere that pervades the language of the play (e.g. 108-9, 120-21, 221-2, 783, 795, 915-17, 1032). As the truth emerges, the use of interrogation, formalized as stichomythia, to build dramatic suspense becomes more insistent (note e.g. the repetition of "how" at 1009, 1015, 1019), until it culminates in Oidipous' discovery of the whole truth (1169-85).

The prologue ends with the arrival of the chorus of Theban elders. Their entry-song (the parodos) consists of three strophic pairs. It opens by invoking one triad of divinities (Athena, Artemis and Apollo), and closes with another (Apollo, Artemis and Dionysos). The use of triads in religious, mythic and magical contexts is common, but threesomes will turn out to have special significance in this play (cf. below, p. 114). The prayer form allows the chorus to reiterate, in intensely emotional lyric mode, the horrors of the plague that the priest has already described, once again using interlaced images of sterility and warfare, fire and disease. In addition to the sterility that mars the beginning of the life cycle, the chorus focuses on its end, singing of funeral pyres and souls fleeing into the sunset (174-7). They also identify the plague with Ares, god of war (and supposedly a protector of Thebes), who carries off men in their prime (190-96). Like warfare, the plague affects men and women in complementary ways. In war, men die in their prime and women (of all ages) mourn for them (178-84). But the very rites of mourning, which should consecrate the end of life, are disrupted by the enormous numbers of the dying, who are flying away like flames (174-81). At the same time fire, which stands for fever, warfare and death, is also a purifying divine force, envisaged as lightning in the hand of Zeus (199-202) or as Dionysos' and Artemis' torches (207-215). This is the "cure," that the Theban noblemen pray for—but it will be a destructive one (compare *Ant.* 1141-3). The gods will indeed save the city, but at a high price to its ancestral rulers.

Oidipous re-emerges from the palace as if he were himself the answer to the chorus' prayer (216). He pronounces a solemn and public curse, and a proclamation of banishment, on Laios' killer, whoever he may be (223-251). In making this pronouncement, Oidipous is in line with the procedures of Athenian law for cases where a murderer was unknown. A proclamation like this one, forbidding the killer to participate in customary rites, could be made by an official called the *basileus* ('king'). But it could also be made by the dead person's next-of-kin. Oidipous, though he does not know it, has the standing to make such a proclamation in both capacities. Unbeknownst to himself or the chorus (though not the audience), he is in fact cursing and banishing himself. These ironies are brought out very heavily by Sophocles (see esp. 219-23, 249-51, 259-68 and cf. 137-40). The oracle, as reported by Kreon, spoke of either exile or execution as remedies for the pollution causing the plague (100-101). These two options again echo Athenian legal practice, whereby death or exile were the normal punishments for intentional homicide, and exile for unintentional. But Oidipous' curse speaks only of banishment. By making no mention of the death penalty, Sophocles sharpens the applicability of the king's pronouncement to his own ultimate fate.

When the chorus suggest sending for the blind old prophet Teiresias, Oidipous shows again that he is one step ahead, since he has already summoned the prophet, who is on his way (284-9). Like Oidipous, Teiresias has rescued the city in the past, and when he enters, Oidipous addresses him with the respect due to a figure of divine insight, supplicating him to "save" the city in a way that evokes the priest's attitude towards himself in the prologue (303-4, 312, 326-7). This sets up a parallelism between the two men, and the exchange that follows exhibits a complex interplay of authority and equality between two kinds of power and two kinds of intelligence. Both men, each in their own way, "have understanding yet [do] not benefit from it" (316-7), Oidipous because his intelligence cannot save him from the awful truth, Teiresias because his divinely-inspired knowledge brings him no personal profit. For both these reasons, Teiresias is initially reluctant to speak the truth. Oidipous is understandably angered by this stalling. Teiresias has the knowledge to save the city, yet is witholding it, and Oidipous is above all a king who cares for his people. It is hard for him to see what possible motive, other than treason, the prophet might have for refusing to impart his wisdom. But it is also reasonable for Teiresias to be offended by Oidipous' angry tone. This provokes him to do just what Oidipous thinks he wants, namely to tell him the truth. In the course of an enraged stichomythic exchange he reveals that Oidipous is himself the murderer of Laios and even hints at the incest with his mother (352-3, 362, 366-8).

This seems to confirm the king's suspicions of disloyalty, and drives him to denounce the prophet in more extreme terms. The language he employs implicitly links Teiresias with Oidipous' old enemy, the Sphinx. Like the Sphinx, the prophet has special kind of enigmatic knowledge deriving from a connection with divinity, and is, on Oidipous' account, a destructive "weaver" of snares (387-8). Such destructive deviousness is frequently represented as a "feminine" trait. And the myths surrounding Teiresias make him a feminized figure. One remarkable feature of his story is that he was turned (albeit temporarily) into a woman, after seeing two snakes copulating and striking them. His blindness may also be viewed symbolically as castration, and hence feminization (cf. below, p. 127). Like such priestesses as Apollo's Pythia, Teiresias has access to irrational and "feminine" but divinely sanctioned sources of knowledge. And the "three legs" on which he walks even evoke the three-footed seat, or tripod, on which the Pythia sat to give her oracles. This mode of knowledge forms a contrast to Oidipous' own supposed "masculine" rationality. Thus Oidipous devalues the "irrational" sources—chattering birds and spluttering entrails—from which the priest derives his insights. He rates his own intellect over Teiresias' because he solved the riddle of the Sphinx, claiming personal credit for his own wit (390-98).

This provokes Teiresias in turn to a more extended denunciation.

He begins by asserting his "equality" with the king, since he views himself as answerable only to Apollo (408-11). Paradoxically, this power derives from his status as Apollo's "slave." This emphasis on personal equality has a democratic resonance, especially in its evocation of the Athenian court system, where the accused was given equal time to defend himself. But there is a more profound way in which the two men will eventually become "equals." At this stage of the play, Oidipous is both physically sighted and famous for his intellectual vision. But as Teiresias puts it later, "you're sighted, but don't see what evil you are in" (413). Teiresias' physical blindness, by contrast, betokens a deeper mode of understanding, close to that of Apollo himself (284-5; cf. 300-302). And when, in a climactic moment, Oidipous taunts Teiresias with blindness "in mind and ears as well as in your eyes," the latter predicts that Oidipous will soon be in this condition himself (371-3). By then, however, he will also, paradoxically, have acquired a degree of intellectual insight that equals Teiresias' own. He too will be a blind old beggar who understands the truth (449-60). They will end up then, in one sense, as equals—both blind, both knowing—but with the power-differential dramatically reversed. In production, both men would probably carry a staff. Oidipous bears the staff of kingly office, with which, unbeknownst to him, he assaulted his own father (810-11). He will lean on it when he returns, blind, at the end of the play, embodying the way in which all mortals are groping in the dark compared to the clear knowledge of the gods. Teiresias, by contrast, enters leaning on the blind man's staff, which signifies physical fraility but also the insight betokened by his blindness. We may wonder whether he also uses it authoritatively, in a dramatic gesture, in his denunciation of Oidipous.

Teiresias gives still one more twist to the theme of equality. Not only will Oidipous as king be made "equal" to the prophet, but Oidipous as father will be "equated" with his children, and even with himself (425-6). In other words, Oidipous will turn out to be his children's "equal" in having been born from the same mother, and "equal to himself" in discovering the true measure of who he is. This theme of equality resonates in various ways throughout the play (cf. e.g. 579-83, 607, 627), most notably in regard to the number of Laios' murderers—a crucial detail on which various speakers vacillate (e.g. 107-8, 122-5, 224, 246-7, 292-6, 843-50). Oidipous will later insist that many could not be equal to one (845)—a remark displaying the rationally calculating mentality that typifies his mode of intelligence (cf. below, p. 111). But he himself will turn out to embody that equation quite literally: the murderer, son, successor and avenger of

Laios are all one person: himself.

Oidipous, of course, has no idea yet of the full import of all this. But though infuriated by the prophet, he is distracted by a casual comment about his parents. When he inquires further, Teiresias responds, "This day will give you birth—and will destroy you too" (438). Oidipous likens this enigmatic response to a riddle, and Teiresias taunts him to solve it, like the riddle of the Sphinx (439-42). The prophet's words do indeed pose the ultimate riddle for Oidipous: the "riddle" of his own identity, the solution to which occupies the rest of the play. Nor are the terms of this "riddle" accidental, with its focus on birth and death in a single day. The extent of a single day is often used in Greek texts as an emblem for the brevity of human life (e.g. *Ant.* 788-9), in contrast to the gods' immortality (cf. e.g. *Ant.* 456-7). The action of particular tragedies is also often limited to a day, in acknowledgment of the fact that a single instant, or "day," can reverse the course of a human life (cf. *OC* 1454-5, *Ant.* 14, 55, 170). This theme echoes through *King Oidipous* as well (see e.g. 351-2, 614-15, 781-2, 1283). But it has additional meaning for this particular play because of the riddle of the Sphinx, which likens the human life-span to a single day.

The solution to the present crisis will once again depend on Oidipous' skill at solving riddles: the riddle of Apollo's prophecies, and the riddle of his own identity posed by Teiresias. As with the Sphinx, this knowledge will be grudgingly extracted by the persistent Oidipous from those reluctant to grant it. And the answer to both riddles will ultimately turn out to be the same as the answer to the riddle of the Sphinx: Oidipous himself. For Oidipous is emblematic of the human race as a whole, whose identity shifts from infancy to maturity to old age in the brief space of a metaphorical "day." That "day" of human life is replicated in the dramatic "day" of the play's action. At the outset Oidipous is, as we have seen, to all appearances at the mid-day of human life, but in the course of the play he will symbolically cover all three stages, piecing them together into the story of a whole life, and thus bringing to birth an understanding of his own identity. That identity is, in turn, a conflation of the three life-stages as represented by three normally distinct generations. He belongs not only to his own generation, but to that of his father (whose wife he married) and that of his children (with whom he shares a mother).

The beginning of that story is uncovered much later in the play, with the Corinthian shepherd's account of Oidipous' infancy. One curious detail of his birth story, which seems to have been invented by Sophocles, is especially significant for the Sphinx's riddle. When, as an infant, he was left on the mountain to die, his feet (or perhaps ankles) were pierced through and joined with some kind of metal pin—the mutilation that supposedly gave him his name (1034-6). Though historically classical Athenians did expose unwanted children to die, it was not normal to mutilate their feet in this way. The most "logical" explanation for such a practice would be to prevent the baby from crawling to safety.[1] But children were exposed as newborns, when they are not yet able to crawl. The significance of the detail is thus more symbolic than literal. It not only suggests the crippling nature of Oidipous' circumstances, but recalls the riddle of the Sphinx, in which a crawling baby signifies the "morning" of human life. The piercing of his feet was designed both to thwart that beginning and to prevent him from growing into an adult man who walks on both legs. (The word for "two-footed" in the Sphinx's riddle (*dipous*) strikingly echoes Oidipous' own name.) The end of the play, by contrast, will produce the destruction of the man he was, and show him to us walking on "three feet" with a blind man's cane, which betokens both physical weakness and prophetic insight.

Teiresias expands on his "riddle" with a remarkably explicit statement of the truth (447-62). It is a dramatically bold move on the poet's part to confront the supremely intelligent Oidipous so bluntly with the truth, and yet have him disbelieve it. It is bold because there is a risk of making Oidipous look foolish, thus undermining the supreme intelligence that is crucial to his story. For this reason, some editors think that Oidipous should exit at 456, while Teiresias speaks to his departing back. But this would dull the impact of the scene, whose central point is that the most rational human being is capable of blindness in the face of truth. Even the most intelligent man in the world can be an ignorant fool when confronted with divine wisdom from a source that does not make sense in normal human terms. The whole scene—indeed the whole play—turns on the question of sound thinking or understanding (*phronein* 302, 316, 403, 462). This and other *phron-* words in Greek have a broad semantic scope, ranging from intellectual capacity to clinical sanity, moral soundness and good sense, and recurs throughout the play, notably in Oidipous' confrontation with Kreon (512, 524-9, 549-52, 570, 601, 626-8; cf. also e.g. 664, 691-2, 1066). The scene between Oidipous and Teiresias provides a dramatic staging of the gulf

---

1   Another rationalization that is sometimes used is that the mutilation is an (unsuccessful) attempt to discourage anyone from rescuing the baby. But this scarcely accounts for its specificity. A different type of explanation is that it was intended to hobble the ghost of the child, which might be angry and seek revenge.

between two modes of understanding: divine and human. The inability of even the most intelligent of mortals to understand the divinely-inspired truth is reinforced by the way in which Teiresias is given the final word, reducing even the powerful Oidipous to silence. The prophet's exit speech ends with the words "understanding" and "skill" (462), signaling his moment of dramatic triumph.

Oidipous is, of course, mistaken in his denigration of the prophet's skills. But this does not in itself make him impious or deserving of censure. In drama and legend oracles always come true, just as exposed babies are always found and scars are always significant (compare below, p. 122). But in the real Greek world priests and prophets were not all viewed as equally prestigious or credible. There were many kinds of prophet, priest and miracle-monger, and some of them (such as the beggar-priests of the eastern mother-goddess Cybele, to whom Oidipous alludes at 388) were viewed by many people—especially the more educated—as money-grubbing charlatans deserving of suspicion and contempt. There were many spurious oracles in circulation. And even oracles from the most respected sources, like Delphi, were typically confusing and open to varying interpretations, which meant that their priests and diviners were not immune from suspicions of trickery. Oracles could also be manipulated for political purposes. Of particular concern to fifth-century Athenians was the fact that the Delphic oracle favored their enemy, Sparta, in the Peloponnesian War (see Thucydides 1.118.3, 2.54). Skepticism about oracles and the traditional gods had been in the air since at least the time of the poet-philosopher Xenophanes some fifty years earlier, and is reflected in other Athenian writers of the fifth century. The reliability of prophecies and oracles was therefore a contemporary issue for Sophocles and his audience.

Even the most faithful believer in prophecies knew that they might be fulfilled in unexpected, non-literal or symbolic ways, in history as well as myth (see e.g. Thucydides 2.17.2). This attitude is exemplifed in Oidipous' reaction to the death of Polybos. If Polybos died out of grief for his absent son, then Oidipous will have "caused" his death in a fashion that, while sad, is morally innocuous (964-72). Jokasta points out that the prophecy of incest might be fulfilled in an equally innocuous fashion, for example through a dream (980-82). It is worth noting in this connection that such dreams are not given a Freudian "Oedipal" coloring in the play, or in antiquity generally. Though often connected with autocratic rule, they are not viewed as specially significant or worrying, but trivial or even optimistic. Indeed, some have thought that Sophocles is alluding to a specific story told by the historian Herodotus: the former Athenian tyrant Hippias dreamed that he had sex with his mother and took this to mean that he would regain power in his motherland; but the dream was fulfilled in an utterly trivial fashion, when he lost a tooth in Athenian soil (Herodotus 6.107). Not only does the dream arouse no anxiety in itself, but neither of these interpretations concerns literal incest.

It is therefore neither impious nor unreasonable—although it is mistaken—for Oidipous to doubt Teiresias' allegations. At the same time, the hasty suspicions of bribery and treachery that Oidipous displays both here and elsewhere (124-5, 137-40, 380-89, 532-42, 960) are characteristic of an absolute ruler, or *turannos*: the word in the title of this play translated as "king."[2] This term, though it eventually gives rise to our word "tyranny," is not intrinsically pejorative. In tragedy, there is nothing intrinsically wrong with being an absolute king: this is the world of legend, not Athenian democracy. Accordingly, other characters address Oidipous as *turannos* (513-14, 924), and both he and other characters use this word, and the related word *turannis*, to refer non-pejoratively to his rule (380, 535, 541, 587-8, 593, 1095). Historically, a *turannos* is an absolute ruler who has taken power through his own efforts rather than by inheriting it (cf. 540-42). Such rulers needed to be energetic, intelligent, and bold, and might have more reason than others to be suspicious of usurpation. The Greek world, including Athens, had known a number of such "tyrants" who ruled often—though not always—in beneficial ways. But in *King Oidipous*, even Laios, a legitimate hereditary king, is referred to in such language without disrespect (128, 799, 1043). The person who entitled this play *Oidipous Turannos*—whether or not it was Sophocles—did not thereby intend to disparage the king as a tyrant or dictator. Only once in this play is the word unequivocally pejorative (873), though there may also be hints of this coloring elsewhere (e.g. 408).

At the same time, democratic Athenians constructed their own political identity in large part by contrasting themselves with other, more autocratic Greek states, and with the absolute rulers whom they associated with the non-Greek or "barbarian" east. Their own tyrannicides from the previous century were celebrated in song and story, and the prayers that opened the democratic asssembly

---

2   Aristotle refers to the play simply as *Oidipous*, so this was presumably the original title The word *turannos* must have been added at some point to distinguish it from Sophocles' other Oidipous play, *Oidipous at Colonus*. The more familiar title *Oedipus Rex* is a Latin translation of *Oidipous Turannos*.

included a curse on anyone trying to restore the kingship. The *turannos* also takes on, in many Athenian contexts, the coloration of a figure who is enviable for his power, but is assumed to abuse that power in order to benefit himself and his friends, committing the most outrageous crimes in the process. This is conveyed at its most extreme by Plato, when he describes the *turannos* as a man in the grip of uncontrollable lust, who robs and assaults his father and wrecks his country, and whom the people want to expel as a parricide (*Republic* 568e-9b, 573c-6b, 615cd). Incest is also often attributed to tyrants, as a token of the extremity of their behavior. Oidipous' status as an absolute ruler is potentially disturbing, because of the kinds of behavior to which such persons are prone, if only by virtue of the power derived from their status. The exact degree to which Oidipous resembles such a ruler is therefore significant in trying to gauge the impact his character may have had on the play's intended audience.

Oidipous is (wrongly) believed by all to be a non-hereditary king of Thebes, who gained power through his own initiative. Although they do not yet know it, this involved killing the legitimate king in a dubiously lawful fashion (below, p. 116). And he has many attributes associated with a *turannos* in the pejorative sense in history and literature. Besides being impulsive, hot-tempered and suspicious of treachery and bribery, he threatens the shepherd with torture (see 1154 with note; cf. also 1166). Such physical mistreatment is often presented as a tyrannical trait (compare *Ant.* 306-9). But it would probably not shock an Athenian audience, since the shepherd is a slave, and slaves could only give testimony in Athenian courts under torture. More serious is the fact that Oidipous comes close to threatening Teiresias with similar treatment (402-3). In other respects, however, he shows a "democratic," non-tyrannical outlook. He comes out to meet his people in person (6-7), tells Kreon to speak out in front of everyone (93-5), and calls a public assembly (143-4). He seeks divine guidance and is eager for advice from others, including the chorus. Moreover his "tyrannical" traits are to a certain extent inseparable from the qualities that make him a great ruler: his decisiveness and vigor have brought him success in the past (618-21; contrast the cautious Kreon: 616-7). He cares above all for the welfare of his people, and they in turn treat him with nothing but love, respect and gratitude.

Most importantly, Oidipous' "tyrannical" character traits are never in fact translated into tyrannical action. Particularly significant here is the way in which he backs down from his threats against Kreon in response to persuasion by Jokasta and the chorus. Oidipous belongs to a character-type often referred to as the "Sophoclean hero," distinguished by its stubbornness and refusal to defer to the wishes of others (see esp. Knox 1964). As Kreon says of his brother-in-law, he has a harsh nature that hates to yield (673-5). Yet he does in fact yield in this instance, even though he sees sparing Kreon as equivalent to his own death or exile (657-8, 669-71). This acquiescence is also based in part on the chorus' appeals to the well-being of the city as a whole (665, 685; cf. 635-6). Oidipous is still the compassionate king who puts his people's well-being before his own.

There is a definite contrast here between Oidipous and certain kings in other tragedies, including Sophocles' other "Theban" plays, who show some of the same traits yet are distinctly more "tyrannical." For example, he resembles Kreon, who is king in *Antigone*, in his anger at Teiresias, his initial refusal to listen (543-6), his desire to punish with death a relative who he thinks has betrayed him (551-2, 623), and his insistence on on the prerogatives of rule, as well as its responsibilities (628-9). Yet these similarities are ultimately superficial. Unlike Kreon in *Antigone*, Oidipous is angered not by the prophet's advice, but by his refusal to provide it. His suspicions of Kreon are not entirely implausible, since it was Kreon who brought the oracle from Delphi, who suggested sending for Teiresias (288, 555-6), who has a long-standing relationship with the prophet, in contrast to the "newcomer" Oidipous (cf. 561-9), and who will inherit the throne if Oidipous loses it. Moreover, in marked contrast to the Kreon of *Antigone*, he is quickly dissuaded from hasty tyrannical behavior by those close to him.

It is also worth comparing Oidipous with his own sons, Eteokles and Polyneikes, as they are portrayed in Oidipous at Colonus. Eteokles and Polyneikes fulfill many of Plato's criteria for the tyrannical character. Specifically, they neglect the well-being of their father and their patrimony (Thebes), thus failing in their obligation as family members and as rulers. Oidipous too is gradually revealed, in *King Oidipous*, as a *turannos* in this sense—someone who violates the ties of family and brings disaster on his city and himself. But again the differences are crucial: as Oidipous himself will argue in Oidipous at Colonus, he did these deeds entirely unintentionally. And of course, in *King Oidipous* he also saves his city for a second time by uncovering the truth, at great cost to himself, whereas his sons will attempt to destroy each other at the city's expense.

The confrontation between king and prophet is followed by the first stasimon—the second choral song. The chorus' reaction to Teiresias' words is a confused foreboding (483-9). Their inability to understand or believe Teiresias' pronouncement of the truth provides retrospective plausibility to Oidipous' own failure to see the point, and at the same time equates him in this respect with more ordinary mortals. The chorus have, of course, heard Teiresias declare that the killer is Oidipous himself. But they cannot makes sense of the idea. This is because they are assuming a normal human motivation for murder—a blood-feud between two families. Since they know of no such feud, they are at a loss as to why Oidipous should have murdered Laios (483-97). In the absence of any "reasonable" explanation or clear proof, even these pious, conventional noblemen prefer to reserve judgment regarding the reliability of the prophet—who is, after all, a mere mortal himself—and remain loyal to the king who has saved the city in the past (498-512).

At the same time, the chorus' speculative picture of the unknown killer is unintentionally appropriate to Oidipous. They speak of Apollo "leaping" on the guilty man (471; cf. 263, 1311), and imagine him lurking in forests and wilderness, isolated from human life (476-7). This prefigures the narrative of Oidipous' abandonment in the mountains (717-19), his optimistic speculation that he is in some sense a child of nature (1080-83), and his final desire for expulsion from human society back to Mount Cithaeron (1451-3). The chorus also declare that for the killer to escape, he must have strong, healthy feet (467-9); instead, he is like a bull with a crippled foot who wanders in an attempt to escape the prophecies from the Delphic oracle (478-81)—just as we know Oidipous, with his scarred feet, has spent his adult life wandering to avoid fulfilling the prophecy given him by that same oracle (795; cf. also 693). The chorus envisage the oracles flying round the fugitive like a flock of birds, or perhaps insects buzzing around the bull to which he is likened (482). The image evokes both the flocks of dead souls from the parodos (174-7), and the Keres, winged goddesses of death and retribution (472). The chorus' words also echo Teiresias' prediction of a curse "with awful foot" that will drive Oidipous forth (418-19). Just as he is both the riddle and its solution, he is the prey as well as its hunter, the curse as well as its victim (and its eventual alleviator).

The picture of the wild bull has further implications for Oidipous' story. Like Oidipous, the bull is emblematic of the wandering outsider poised between civilization and savagery (cf. *Ant.* 350-51). Unlike other fierce wild animals—such as a lion—the bull is not intrinsically destructive to human civilization, since it serves a valuable purpose when domesticated. But it has no useful function in itself, unless it is properly integrated into human culture. Similarly Oidipous, who starts out as the embodiment of cultural and civic life, the successfully incorporated outsider, will turn out to embody the perversion of human cultural and reproductive life as embodied in the family. At the end of the play, when the full enormity of that perversion is apparent, Oidipous "ranges about" the house (1255)—the same word used for the wild bull by the chorus (476). And when he finds Jokasta hanged, he bellows like a bull (1265). Such linguistic echoes in the choral odes should not be taken as conscious hints from the chorus, who are unaware of the relevant details of Oidipous' story, but as part of the fabric of irony and human ignorance created by the dramatist.

As the chorus end their song, Kreon re-enters in order to defend himself from Oidipous' charge of treachery. This accusation is, of course, no more than an inference from the supposed treachery of Teiresias. As such it provides us with an example of Oidipous' quick wit, his ability to put two and two together, to "add up" the evidence and infer the truth. This kind of calculative, rational intelligence is Oidipous' great strength, as the play's language often reflects (e.g. 73, 461, 561, 795, 839-47, 915-16, 963, 1019, 1110-13). It is not a coincidence that the riddle of the Sphinx, and its solution, required an understanding of numbers and their symbolic meanings, which "add up" to the meaning of a human life. It is this ability to make inferences that eventually leads Oidipous to the truth, in large part by solving two numerical "riddles": the meaning of the place where three roads meet, and the equivalence of one and many murderers (above, p. 103). But such wit can also be misguided. In the present case, Oidipous has put two and two together to make five.

Oidipous' hostility towards Kreon escalates during their stichomythic exchange, in which a combative and sarcastic tone is conveyed by the echoing of phrases and words from line to line (cf. e.g. 543-52, 569-70). At the same time, the exchange shows us the rational basis of Oidipous' accusations (555-73). These have some plausibility, thus exemplifying the unfortunate fact that what appears both rational and plausible to the logical human mind may in fact be far from the truth. As Oidipous acutely points out, Teiresias did not accuse him of the murder at the time it occurred (562-8). This kind of rational argument, based on what a person should plausibly have done in a certain situation, is eminently suitable to a court of law. Such arguments were intrinsic to the theory and practice of rhetoric in fifth-century Athens. As such they were valuable, since rhetoric was an important route to power in Athenian democracy, but at the same time deeply suspect, in so far as they were thought of as dangerously manipulative. Arguments based on mere verbal logic, whether that logic was valid or specious, were viewed with deep ambivalence (witness the hostility aroused by Socrates). In any case, as this play makes so clear, religious and mythic "logic" work differently. Oidipous' argument from probability takes him in entirely the wrong direction.

Kreon starts the scene in a sympathetic light (513-22). In response to Oidipous' "tyrannical" suspicions of bribery and treachery, he adopts a "democratic" posture, appealing, like Teiresias before him, to the importance of "equal" speech and persuasion (543-4; cf. 606-7, 630). In contrast to his counterpart in *Antigone*, he refrains from transgressive religious attitudes (contrast 1424-31 with *Ant.* 1039-43), uses rhetorical arguments based on plausible motivation, and declines to speak when he is ignorant (569).[3] He even speaks to Oidipous very much as Haimon—Kreon's own son—addresses his father in the earlier play (*Ant.* 737-9; cf. *OT* 630, also 54-7). And his self-defence is effective in demonstrating the absence of real evidence behind Oidipous' reasoning (cf. 608-9). At the same time, it reveals some less appealing aspects of Kreon's character. Though innocuous enough, he is essentially unheroic and scarcely admirable. Oidipous is not so far wrong in suspecting that Kreon desires power, or that he wants to exert it without getting into personal trouble (cf. 706). He seeks the privileges of power without its responsibilities. As he puts it himself, if he really were king, that role would place constraints on the satisfaction of his own desires (590-92). His motivation is basically self-serving (cf. 594-5). The chorus remark aptly that Kreon has spoken well for someone taking care to protect himself (616-7).

All this stands in sharp contrast to the way Oidipous himself, in the prologue, takes upon his own shoulders the suffering of his people. The quiet life praised by Kreon contrasts with the "competitive and highly envied life" that Oidipous speaks of as the lot of kings (381). Kreon prefers to sleep peacefully, in contrast to Oidipous' wakefulness on behalf of the citizens (585; cf. 65). This makes him deficient not only in heroic terms, but also by democratic standards, since the power he wants to exert is based on personal contacts rather than public acclaim (cf. 596-8), and manipulation rather than openness (cf. 91-4). In Euripides' play *Hippolytos*, the hero claims similarly that he prefers to be the power behind the throne rather than to sit on it (*Hipp.* 1017-20). But unlike Kreon, Hippolytos is a young man only just reaching manhood. His rhetoric suggests

---

3   As in *Antigone*, however, he has a penchant for sententious utterances (87-8, 110-11, 600, 609-15; compare *Ant.* 175-90).

that he is resisting the process of maturation, refusing to grow up, take responsibility and become engaged in community life in this and other ways. It is even less appropriate to a man of Kreon's social standing.

The two men's quarrel is defused by the arrival of Jokasta (634), who, as Oidipous' wife and Kreon's sister, is well placed to mediate between them. Although women in democratic Athens did not have the public visibility of a queen of the legendary period, nonetheless, like Jokasta, they served the function of linking together, through marriage, the family of their birth and that of their husband. In myth, women are more familiar as a source of strife between men. Jokasta illustrates, by contrast, the positive side of women's social function as a mediator between men's households. But her intervention also has more sinister overtones. Unbeknownst to any of them, the two families between which she is mediating—her birth family and marital family—are not in fact two, but one. And she herself lies at the heart of that unity, in her incestuous role as Oidipous' wife/mother.

This is brought out through subtle ironies of character. Jokasta's assertive tone towards her husband and adult brother is unusual for a Greek wife, and carries the unmistakable suggestion of a mother reprimanding her children (634-8). Though obedient to her husband, as a good Greek wife should be (862), she also adopts the tone of a comforting and indulgent mother, concerned for her child's well-being and happiness and anxious that he should not be over-excited (707-25, 914-5). Conversely, Oidipous is not only affectionate towards his wife (cf. 950), but treats her with a degree of intimacy and respect that is extremely unusual for a Greek man towards his wife (579-80, 700-701, 769-73, 800). Even the chorus assumes that Jokasta exerts personal authority over Oidipous, expecting her to take him into the house—a reversal of the normal male-female relationship, in which the husband "leads" the bride to his house in marriage (678-9; cf. 861-2, 950-51). A male-female relationship that might seem to many modern readers refreshingly close and egalitarian is, by ancient Greek standards, a departure from social norms, hinting at the much more drastic violation of such norms that lies beneath the surface.

After separating the two men, Jokasta attempts to reassure Oidipous by dismissing the validity of Teiresias' prophecies. She is a pious woman, who has no doubt about the gods' ability to make their wishes known (724-5; cf. also 646-7, 698, 911-13, 1060). She therefore does not reject prophecy as such, but rather its reliability as filtered through human intermediaries (707-25). Her later dismissal of prophecy may seem more extreme (851-8), but it is not incompatible

with the perfectly respectable view that an oracle might be fulfilled
in symbolic ways, such as dreaming—a possibility she will herself
suggest to Oidipous (980-82; cf. above, p. 106-7). Her skepticism
concerning the literal truth of oracles is therefore by no means impious
in itself. And she has what seems to be good evidence for it: an
oracle once received by her former husband, Laios, apparently went
unfulfilled (707-25; cf. 851-8). Oidipous himself will agree that Jokasta's
scepticism of oracles on these grounds seems well-founded (859).

The prophecy in question is, of course, eerily symmetrical with
that received by Oidipous himself (cf. 790-94). Common sense might
suggest that this should alert Oidipous to the truth. Other aspects of
Jokasta's tale might also seem to make it obvious that Oidipous is
himself the killer, in particular the reference to the baby's mutilated
feet (718). It is important to bear in mind, however, that Oidipous
does not know he was a foundling. His failure to associate this event
with his own scarred feet is tolerably credible, since Jokasta's word
'yoke' (718) could indicate no more than tying the feet together. More
importantly, however, canons of common-sense realism are rarely
appropriate to the characters of Greek tragedy. Oidipous' failure
to connect the two narratives is more pathetic than foolish. For the
audience, this pathos arises from our own superior knowledge,
which places us in a privileged position vis à vis Oidipous—a
position resembling that of the gods towards mortals generally and
towards this exemplar of the human race in particular.

Once again, words of reassurance produce the opposite of their
intended effect, as Jokasta's passing reference to a place where three
roads meet prompts Oidipous to starts wondering if he is, after all,
the killer (726-7). This fatal spot receives considerable emphasis in
the text (716, 730, 733, 801, 1398). It lies at the center of Oidipous'
wanderings, both literal and intellectual, and has an array of symbolic
associations. To begin with, the three roads evoke the three stages of
the human path through life embodied in the riddle of Sphinx. More
obviously, arriving at a fork in the road is a metaphor for facing
a choice that will determine the nature and course of one's life.
Such a choice is a token of self-knowledge and identity. The most
famous example from the fifth century concerns the hero Herakles.
Travelling as a young man, Herakles reaches a fork in the road where
Virtue stands on once side and Vice on the other, and must choose
which path to take. By choosing the path of Virtue, Herakles creates,
confirms and acknowledges his heroic nature. As this kind of story
implies, the theme of the meeting of three roads is also a theme about
doubleness, since the traveller along one road is faced by a choice
between two (the "fork" in the road at 733).

In literal dramatic terms, the junction of three roads echoes the structure of the tragic stage, with its central doorway flanked by two side entrances. Like Oidipous at the crossroads, the palace stands between the world outside Thebes and the city itself, between civilization and wilderness. As such it embodies the hidden world of the female, as opposed to the city and the outside world, both of which are arenas of public male activity. The parting in the road is also often given a sexual symbolic meaning, linking Oidipous' parricide to his incest with his mother. This helps to make sense of the way the incest is oddly present in his most detailed description of the spot where he killed his father. Oidipous encounters Laios at a place in the road too narrow for them to pass each other—a place symbolically identified with Jokasta's sexuality. The location of the parricide is described with a sexually suggestive emphasis on its natural surroundings: it is hidden, narrow and wooded. In Greek texts the natural world is frequently the locus of transgressive sexual encounters. Moreover Oidipous speaks of this spot "remembering" the incest as well as the murder (1398-1403). The resulting conflation of incest and murder evokes the "two-pronged goad" of the curse on Oidipous (417-18), itself reminscent of the goad with which Laios strikes him (809), the "two hands" with which he kills his father (821), the injury inflicted by Laios on his two feet by "yoking" them (718), and the pair of brooches with which he stabs his two eyes with his own two hands (1268, 1318-21). These persistent dualisms underline the way in which roles that should be two have become one: a son has become his mother's husband, and children siblings of their father (see esp. 457-60, 1207-13, 1280-81, 1361, 1403-7).

The mention of the three-pronged road sends Oidipous' thoughts "wandering" back to his past (727), with its literal wandererings. Ironically believing that the truth is now "transparent" (754), he proceeds to give his wife—and us—a vivid narrative, epic in tone, of the events leading up to Laios' death (774-833). This speech, in which Oidipous tells the story of his life as he understands it, lies literally at the center of the play. And it is rich with ironies of character. We already know from Jokasta that there is a physical resemblance between father and son (743)—a fact that in a normal, healthy family would be a cause for celebration, since it testifies to the chastity of the mother and the legitimacy of the paternal line, and raises the expectation that the son will live up to his father in other ways as well. From Oidipous' account we discover that they are also similar in character—imperious, impulsive, aggressive and quick-tempered—and that this very similarity led to the older man's death. The kind of familial closeness that is desirable and admirable in a healthy family and society becomes a token of disaster in this family where intimacy has turned in upon itself.

How culpable is Oidipous—in Sophocles' account—for killing the stranger and his attendants at the crossroads? This is a finely balanced issue. The poet has gone to great lengths to qualify the deed as one which, though perhaps reprehensible, is not really criminal. The deed is presented as disturbingly violent and lawless, especially for a man who is now king. But the picture is not of a criminal act so much as a brawl involving escalating violence on both sides. The assault was provoked by Laios' attack on Oidipous, which was a response to Oidipous hitting the driver, which was in turn a response to their attempt to push him out of the road. Retaliation was a familiar value in Greek culture. Indeed, great heroes, starting with Achilles in the *Iliad*, often engage, in the name of justice, in acts of retaliation that seem excessive by modern standards. In classical Athens, homicide in self-defence was lawful and went unpunished, provided that one could prove that the victim had struck the first blow, and that the blow was deemed murderous in intent. In this case, Laios clearly did strike the blow, but whether it was of a kind that would justify homicide in retaliation is entirely unclear. Social factors conditioning an audience's response are also ambiguous. According to aristocratic, traditional ethics, a younger man would be expected to give way to an older man who appeared to be of higher status and was accompanied by a herald. On the other hand, contemporary Athenian values of democracy and equality are on the side of Oidipous, who resists the royal presumption of Laios' kingly entourage. Oidipous' own distress at this moment in the play, severe as it is, is caused not by the fact that he killed this stranger (which does not trouble him in itself), but by the possibility that he killed the king whose wife he has now married, caused the plague on Thebes, and is subject to the appalling curse that he himself has laid upon the killer. Neither he nor anyone else shows any concern for the other, putatively innocent people that he also killed.

Some modern readers have mistakenly assumed that Oidipous' quick temper, which leads to Laios' death, is a "fatal flaw" of character for which he is being punished by the gods. This familiar but misleading phrase derives ultimately from Aristotle, who declares in his *Poetics* that the central character in a tragedy falls because of a *megalē hamartia* or "great error" (1453a15-16). But *hamartia* does not mean "character flaw." In its original context, the phrase is more accurately translated as "huge mistake." In Oidipous' case, the mistake is quite obviously his ignorance of who his parents really are. And this is not, by any standard, a crime or flaw of character.

This does not mean Oidipous' character is spotless. Like his father, he is impetuous and sometimes ill-tempered. Such defects are frequent corollaries of an otherwise admirable capacity for bold, decisive action. But Oidipous' downfall is not a punishment for these minor defects of character. If all quick-tempered people were to suffer the fate of Oidipous, the world would indeed be a horrific place. Nor is there any sign within the play that the gods are angry with Oidipous for this reason. When he calls himself hateful to the gods (816, 1346-7, 1519), this does not mean they have punished him for a moral transgression. The Greek gods are not essentially moral beings, and can mistreat mortals for a wide variety of reasons which may remain entirely mysterious to their victims.

Nor is it plausible to view Oidipous' fate as a punishment for any other failing. If parricide and incest are the "crimes" for which he is being punished, they cannot also be the punishment. He himself views the parricide and incest as signs of divine hatred, not as a cause of it. He is certainly not being punished for fleeing the oracle about his parents (794-8). By trying to invalidate it, he is not showing disbelief in the gods and their power (rather the opposite). He is also, in practice, increasing the chance that the prophecies could be fulfilled in some unexpected or symbolic way that may leave him innocent. Nor is the outcome a punishment for killing an older man or marrying an older woman. Since Oidipous is convinced that he knows who his parents are, the worst that he could be accused of is foolishness. In any case, this suggestion replaces the logic of myth with the logic of everyday common sense, which is rarely a useful criterion for judging the behavior of heroic characters. On the other hand, the fact that what happened is Oidipous' "destiny" (*moira* 376, 1458; cf. 713, 863) does not remove his personal responsibility for any of the choices he makes in working out that destiny. Destiny or "fate," in Greek thinking, denotes not a coercive force but the shape of the life that one happens to live out, which is known in advance by the gods, but in which we remain fully responsible for our actions. Moreover the action of the play itself—the discovery of that destiny—is not predicted or controlled by the gods, but consists in a series of understandable and unconstrained human choices made by its hero.

Though Oidipous' narrative makes it all too clear that he is indeed the killer (813-33), he clings to one remaining straw of hope. Jokasta included the crucial—and crucially misleading—detail that Laios was killed by a gang of robbers (715), not a single man travelling alone. To be sure of the truth, Oidipous must interrogate Laios' slave attendant, the sole survivor of the attack at the crossroads

(836-47). After sending for this crucial eye-witness, Oidipous is reduced to an uncharacteristic state of passivity: he can do nothing but wait (836-7). While he does so, the chorus sing and dance their next song: the notoriously complex and problematic second stasimon.

This song begins with a rhapsodic invocation of piety and the eternal laws of the gods (863-71; cf. *Ant.* 450-60). The first antistrophe develops the implied contrast with human sovereignty by declaring, "outrage gives birth to kings" (873).[4] "King" translates the ambivalent word *turannos* (above, p. 000), whose negative associations are spelled out in the lines that follow. "Outrage" translates *hubris*, a concept that is often misunderstood, and applied improperly or misleadingly to this and other tragedies. Contrary to modern popular usage, *hubris* does not, in general, denote an arrogant attitude towards the gods ("haughtily" in line 884 is a different word). It is not a quality of character, nor is it intrinsically religious. Rather, it standardly refers to excessively violent, abusive, or insulting behavior, which violates another person's proper status. Thus in Athenian law, it refers to mental or physical abuse, including rape, unprovoked assault and certain kinds of verbal insult, directed at another human being as a way of asserting one's own superiority. In tragedy, the word occurs much less frequently than the modern reader might expect. But it is used, for example, in *Antigone,* to denote wilful defiance of the king's authority (*Ant.* 309, 480-83). The gods, of course, do not like such treatment any more than anyone else, and disrespect for their power and status may be severely punished. But *hubris* is not a religious offense per se.

What does it mean, then, to say that *hubris* "gives birth to" autocratic kings or "tyrants"? It could mean that outrageous, violent behavior (his own or that of others) enables a tyrant to take power; or engenders a tyrannical state of mind; or makes people view a king as tyrannical; or makes a previously responsible king into a dictator. There is a strong tradition in Greek moralizing whereby *hubris* leads one to excessive self-indulgence, which is followed by a kind of folly or moral blindness, which in turn results in criminal behavior that is punished by the gods. The chorus give a vivid desciption of such a man, whose tyrannical behavior leads to his own downfall (873-9). They continue with a strongly worded condemnation of such persons, declaring that the gods punish injustice and impiety—by implication,

---

4   Some editors alter the text so that it means "kingship gives birth to outrage," which is simpler in meaning. But simplicity is rarely a good argument for altering the text of choral lyrics, which are dense and complex in their mode of expression.

that of the hubristic tyrant in the preceding stanza (883-96).

The central controversy surrounding this ode concerns how these remarks about piety, *hubris* and tyranny are—or are not—related to Oidipous and his behavior and situation. Certainly, their immediate relevance is obscure. Oidipous has not been impious, nor would piety have saved him from killing Laios. Jocasta has not been impious, merely sceptical of oracles. As we have seen, Oidipous is clearly a *turannos*, and does have certain character-traits associated with a *turannos*, for better but also for worse, in history and literature (above). Moreover the chorus has now heard that he may be the killer of Laios (though no one yet realizes that he was killing his father)—a deed which led, albeit indirectly, to Oidipous' kingship of Thebes, and so might be viewed as "giving birth to" his kingship. The chorus' desire for "purity" (864) may also indicate a concern about the pollution caused by almost any killing. Yet as we have seen, to kill in a street-brawl a stranger who struck the first blow is not *hubris*—at least not under Athenian law.

On the other hand, choral anxiety about *hubris* may have been prompted by something quite different, namely Oidipous' treatment of first Kreon and then Teiresias. To be sure, they are not actually accusing him of tyranny or *hubris*. Indeed they explicitly contrast such behavior with the kind of competitive striving that benefits the city, which they view with approval (880-81). This positive kind of "contest" not only has a democratic resonance (Athenian society was highly competitive), but was clearly exemplifed by Oidipous himself, when he defeated all others—including Teiresias (390-92)—in solving the riddle of the Sphinx. But the chorus does stress the fine line that divides this kind of useful ambition from its negative counterpart. His treatment of Kreon and Teiresias may therefore generate some uneasiness.

Unbeknownst to the chorus, however, Oidipous has indeed violated the "divine laws" against parricide and incest, and in doing so laid hands on what is "untouchable" (892). And as usual, their language has subtle resonances that make their words more pertinent to him than may at first appear. Though nothing in the ode is directed at Oidipous explicitly, its language hints at the deeds he has unknowingly done, especially through the imagery of feet (866, 879), travel (876-8, 883-4)—including travel to Delphi (897-8)—and birth (867, 873). In a particularly striking image, which employs a unique Greek word, the chorus describe the divine laws as "lofty of foot" (866), recalling both Oidipous' own name and the theme of human feet in the Sphinx's riddle. This verbal reminiscence suggests that only gods are truly great, since they are immune from the mortality and fallibility that are part of the human condition, even for an exceptional man and king like Oidipous (866-71).

The chorus end the song by staking their own ritual practice on their trust in divine justice. The famous rhetorical question, "Why should I dance for the gods?" (896), is commonly taken as a metatheatrical allusion. The chorus, who represent Theban citizens praying to their gods, are also Athenian citizens, dancing as theatrical performers in honor of Dionysos, whose priest, along with others, is enthroned in the front row of the audience. In their role as Thebans, the chorus emphatically re-affirm their faith in oracles, and specifically in the veracity of Apollo's oracle at Delphi, declaring that all worship is pointless unless the oracles concerning Laios prove true (897-910). This might seem odd, given the nature of the oracles in question: one would think their fulfilment undesirable for all concerned. But the chorus' anxiety about the veracity of oracles in general does not mean that they would not welcome an innocuous solution, if one were to emerge. As things stand, their central dilemma is how they can retain their faith in these oracles and also in their king.

As if in response to these concerns, Jokasta emerges from the palace with incense and offerings to placate the gods, specifically Apollo (911-23). This entrance forms a contrast with the play's opening scene, with its collective supplication, incense and garlands. As the focus of the play shifts from the public (the plague upon Thebes) to the personal (the identity of Oidipous), a public scene of prayer and supplication is reiterated in the personal actions of a single woman. And the prayer and supplication are no longer to Oidipous, but for him. Jokasta's entrance also makes it clear that despite her earlier scepticism about prophecy, she is a conventionally pious woman. Her scepticism was motivated not by impiety, but by an overriding desire to comfort Oidipous and make sense of the past regarding Laios' oracle. Here again, her concern is for Oidipous' peace of mind, and it is his agitation that prompts her to seek divine assistance. Her report on his mental state indicates that as he comes closer to the truth, he is, in her view, behaving increasingly irrationally (914-17, 922-3).

Jokasta's prayer to Apollo appears to be answered by the arrival of the messenger from Corinth (924), which is both unprepared and unexpected. (He is the only outsider in the play who enters without having been summoned by Oidipous.) The audience has been awaiting Laios' servant (cf. 859-60), and may momentarily think that this is him, since both men are aged shepherds. The Corinthian shepherd has more personality than most "messengers" in Greek tragedy (including the second messenger in this play), and is more engaged both in the plot and its resolution. His news that Oidipous' Corinthian "father" has died of natural causes seems to undermine Apollo's credibility (946-9, 952-3). But once again, a message that seems to bring relief turns out to do the opposite. This is the moment used by Aristotle, in his *Poetics*, to exemplify tragic "reversal" (*peripeteia*) at its best (1452a22-33).

Jokasta concludes from the death of Polybos that since prophecies cannot be trusted, and we are all subject to the rule of the goddess Fortune, it is best for human beings to "take life as it comes" (977-9). But the word translated here as Fortune (*tuchē*) also means "chance." Though in some ways these two concepts may seem like opposites, they are actually two sides of the same coin. "Chance" refers to occurrences that seem accidental or random from the point of view of those who experience them. But such events are by no means random to the gods who cause them. We humans cannot predict, for example, where lightning will strike; but from the point of view of Zeus, who sends the lightning, each such event is caused by divine will and has a purpose. Similarly, from a modern scientific perspective, a lightning-strike that is experienced by its victim as a chance event is by no means random from the perspective of the laws of physics. A central thread of *King Oidipous* is that events that seem random or accidental or coincidental are part of a larger pattern of cause and effect when seen from the point of view of a larger understanding. When Jokasta says we are ruled by Fortune (977-8), and Oidipous calls himself Fortune's child (1080-81), both speak more truly than they know.

This close-knit cohesion of apparently chance events is dramatically enacted as the play unfolds. The messenger thinks he is banishing Oidipous' fear of incest by breaking the news that the Corinthian king and queen were not his birth parents (1016). He knows this because—by chance—he turns out to be the servant who received the baby Oidipous from the Theban shepherd who was assigned the task of exposing him (1022). That shepherd, will turn out, in another dramatically efficient "coincidence," to be the same person as the slave who fled the scene of Laios' death (1051-2), and can therefore identify Oidipous as the killer. The equation of these different bit-players in Oidipous' story is an obvious dramatic economy, but also enacts on a theatrical level the tightening noose of coincidence.

Oidipous' interrogatation of the Corinthian messenger takes him—and us—back still further into the past, to his infancy, or the "morning" of his life. The old shepherd, who served as his "savior" and temporary "father" (1015-20, 1030, 1179, 1456-7), addresses him paternally as "child" (1008, 1030). As "witnesses" to the truth of his narrative he offers Oidipous' own crippled feet, which link him physically to the story of his birth, and provide him with both his name and his true identity (1032-6). Although the "swollen-foot" interpretation of Oidipous name is foremost here, the interpretation "knower of feet" is also relevant. Oidipous' injured feet evoke a motif that occurs in many tragedies: the use of material objects as "recognition-tokens" left with abandoned babies. (The words translated as "clue" at 222 and "evidence" at 710 and 1059 are both suggestive of such tokens.) When the child grows up, these items are used to disclose its true identity to itself and others—most poignantly to the mother who abandoned it in infancy. Oidipous likewise has carried from the cradle the physical evidence that now enables him to be identified by his next of kin—most importantly, his mother, who will be the first to realize the truth.

Oidipous' scarred feet belong to him more intimately, however, than the external birth-tokens, such as a ring or a piece of clothing, that normally accompany exposed infants. His identity has been inscribed on his actual body since his birth—an inscription by means of mutilation that will be reenacted at the end of the play when he puts out his own eyes. (The same Greek word is used for "feet" at 718 and 1032 and for "eye-sockets" at 1270.) In the mythic tradition, feet are often linked with identification. Jason, for example, is recognized by his one bare foot, and gods may be recognized by their feet, even when they are in disguise (*Iliad* 13.71-2). Remarkably often, even the greatest heroes have injured legs or feet (often indicated by the same word in Greek). Achilles, for example, dies from an arrow in his heel, and Philoktetes has a wounded leg. Such physical marks may be used to betoken a person's heroic identity, most famously in the case of Odysseus, who is recognized in Homer by the scar on his leg (*Odyssey* 19.467-75). In classical Athens, however, physical mutilation was associated with outsiders, foreigners, barbarians and slaves, in contrast to the carefully-preserved integrity of the citizen body. This is probably reflected in Oidipous' own attitude towards his scarred feet. When he refers to them as an "insult" (1035), he is referring not only to the indignity of his disfigurement, but to the assumption that his birth was as lowly as that of the shepherd who rescued him, or even worse (cf. 1062-3).

As a token of identity in all these ways, Oidipous' scarring is yet another sign or riddle that he must learn to interpret. Ironically it is Jokasta, the anti-rational, anti-prophetic, "irrational" woman, who discouraged inquiry and counselled living life "as it comes," who solves this "riddle" first—before the rational, intelligent Oidipous can do so (compare 1071 with 1182). In a reversal of their previous roles as optimist and pessimist, insightful and ignorant, respectively, she begs her husband not to persist in inquiry, saying "may you never find out who you are" (1068). She thus serves simultaneously as a witness to the limitations of his understanding, and as a foil to his desire to know the truth about himself at all costs. After all, striving for knowledge is an understandable, even admirable, aspect of human nature. As Aristotle was to put it in the famous opening line of his *Metaphysics*, "All human beings by nature desire to know." There is therefore something counterintuitive about Jokasta's attempt to dissuade him from pursuing it, however understandable that attempt may be under the circumstances. Moreover, despite the failure of intelligent calculation to save Oidipous from his own fate, it does, by bringing him to the truth, succeed in saving Thebes for a second time. Human understanding may be inadequate in comparison with divine, yet it is also an indispensable human excellence, and as such the only intellectual resource available to us most of the time.

Oidipous' "desire to know" is thus a token of his heroic nature. Accordingly, he refuses to be dissuaded by his wife (1056-68). As he puts it, to fail to inquire further would be a rejection of who he really is (1084-5). In contrast to the respect and even deference that he showed Jokasta earlier, he dismisses and insults her for her supposedly "womanly" concerns (1062-3, 1070, 1078-9). His attitude now betrays the typically Greek cultural assumption that women's concerns are more trivial than men's and that they are more subject to strong emotion and lacking in self-control. Jokasta begs him to desist "for his own good"—the typical attitude of a parent towards a dependent child—but he replies that he is tired of such paternalism (or maternalism) from her (1066-7). This defiance of Jokasta's authority as mother is necessary in order for Oidipous to discover that this is who she is. Increased self-assertion is essential to his identity as an independent adult male: it is linked both to his discovery of who he is (1068) and to his final severance from his mother (1071-2). We may compare the behavior of Odysseus' son Telemachos in the *Odyssey*, whose passage to manhood is conveyed in part by a newfound authority over his own mother, whom he commands to be silent and retire to the women's quarters (1.356-59). The language he uses is reminiscent of a husband's to his wife, like the words of Hektor to Andromache in the *Iliad* (6.490-93). Similarly, Oidipous' new attitude towards Jokasta resembles that of an adult man in classical Athens, who would have legal guardianship over both his wife and his widowed mother—Jokasta in both her roles. She exits, now silent, as an Athenian "good wife" ought to be, entering the private, female realm of the house. With her final words, she leaves Oidipous to be "named" or identified only as "unhappy" (1071-2)—the same epithet she earlier used for the infant she left otherwise unnamed (855).

Once again, Oidipous puts two and two together to reach the wrong conclusion, inferring that Jokasta is ashamed of his potentially "evil" or humble birth (1062-3; cf. 1070, 1076-9). This passage well exemplifies the ambiguity in the meaning of the common adjective *kakos*, which can generically be rendered as "bad," but in practice covers a wide range of social, moral and practical deficiences (e.g. 127, 219, 329, 521, 548, 582, 600, 610, 615, 629), and often serves in tragedy as a strong word of condemnation (e.g. 248, 334). (In order to retain some of its strength in this translation, I have usually rendered it as "evil.") Thus Oidipous assumes that Jokasta is concerned about "evil," i.e. humble, birth, whereas she is anxious that he not find out just how "evil," in a very different sense, his birth in fact is (cf. 1397; also 822). Indeed, it is his noble birth that is the problem (cf. 264-8).

Oidipous revels in the idea that he may be "a child of Fortune" and brother to the months that measure the passage of time (1080-83)—a notion that establishes him as a paradigm of human nature in the most optimistic sense (cf. 977). Ironically, of course, these same forces—Fortune and time—are the agents of his downfall. The irony is enhanced by the faithful chorus. In their next song, the brief third stasimon, they develop the conceit that Oidipous is a child of divine and natural forces, more specifically of Cithaeron, the mountain that plays a key role in his life-story and is emblematic of wilderness (1086-96; cf. 421, 1391, 1452). They fantasize that he may be the son of a nymph who had sex with a divinity, such as Pan, Apollo or Dionysos, on the mountainside. This would place him in the company of such great heroes as Achilles and Herakles, who were the offspring of gods and human mothers (or nymphs). It is characteristic of Sophocles to give his choruses such odes of misplaced rejoicing just before disaster strikes—odes that show clearly the limitations of choruses as characters (cf. Introduction, p. 13). Dramatically speaking, the song serves to enhance Oidipous' restoration to joy and confidence, which in turn heightens the impact of his fall. It also intensifies the pathos for the audience (who already know the truth) by inviting us to imagine an impossible alternative universe, in which the name of Oidipous betokens the glory of a "normal" hero instead of the utter degradation with which his name became synonymous.

After this short song the Theban shepherd who witnessed

Laios' murder finally appears (1110). By now we know that he is also the person who transferred the infant Oidipous to the Corinthian shepherd. This makes him the crucial missing link between the quest for Laios' murderer and the quest for Oidipous' identity, which allows the two stories, and the two inquiries, to become one. The importance of his identity is marked dramatically by Oidipous' introductory words, which are characteristically reasonable and calculative in tone (1110-16). If he is to piece together the various paths of inquiry and find the truth that links them, the messenger and herdsman must meet in his presence. All three actors are thus required to be on stage for this climactic moment. Historically, Sophocles was said to have introduced the third actor to the Athenian tragic stage (Introduction, p. 3). But it is unusual for all three actors to engage with each other as intricately as they do here. By doing so they embody and dramatize the need for these three characters to meet in order for Oidipous' life story to be complete.

Like Jokasta, the humble, "ignorant" shepherd sees the truth before the intelligent king, and expresses this awareness through reluctance to speak (1146-51). But under threat from the king, he must finally answer. The moment of truth is at hand for Oidipous. As he faces it, he explicitly takes upon himself the decision to pass from ignorance to knowledge (1169-70). In contrast to the unwitting actions of the past, all human actions within the play are freely chosen in accordance with each agent's character. Above all, there is strong insistence on Oidipous' own freedom of action, which has been highlighted by the attempts of others to dissuade him—attempts he overcame in order to reach this climactic moment. As the dramatic pressure increases, the two speakers start dividing single lines between them (1173-6). Oidipous' questions diminish in length while the shepherd's responses grow longer. They thus enact theatrically, on a miniature scale, the way Oidipous' control of his destiny diminishes as the past, embodied in the shepherd, reasserts itself. With the shepherd's climactic words, "ill-destined was your birth," he sees the accuracy of the prophecy, and in doing so solves the riddle of his own identity (1181-2).

As the audience has known from the outset, Apollo's oracle spoke the literal truth, despite Oidipous' efforts to escape it. This does not mean that human agency is impossible or pointless, or that human beings are mere puppets of the gods. The concepts of "free will" and "determinism"—and the problems they raise—were not developed until long after Sophocles' time. An oracle predicting future events does not make those events take place. Prophecies like those received by Laios and Oidipous are simply predictions. If they are truthful predictions (as they always are in drama), then they are logically unavoidable and will "necessarily" come true. It is in this sense that Oidipous "must" kill his father and marry his mother (792, 826, 854, 995-6). But this is not a denial of human responsibility. For example, when Jesus in the Gospel predicts that Peter will deny him three times, and the prophecy is fulfilled, this does not mean Peter had no choice in the matter; instead, Peter bewails his own weakness after the fact (*Matt.* 26.75). As such stories make clear, divine foreknowledge and human free will can in principle coexist. The truthfulness of prophecy provides us with the dubious "consolation" of a divine order outside our understanding whereby all these things can be predicted and understood by the gods despite the inadequacy of human calculation.

The climactic moment of discovery is marked by another short choral song (the fourth stasimon). This complements the preceding ode by once again using Oidipous as an exemplar for all humanity, but this time with the opposite valence. The ode is marked by a series of verbal repetitions. The double repetition of "yours" in 1192-4 is the most striking of these, and powerfully expresses the chorus's shocked incredulity that Oidipous of all people should have turned out to be so unfortunate. As the song ends, the second messenger emerges from within the palace. In keeping with the general (though not universal) Greek tragic convention of describing rather than showing deeds of violence, he tells us what has taken place inside. Indeed, he draws attention to that convention by asserting that the "vision" (*opsis*) of their suffering is the most painful part of the affair (1238-9; cf. 1224). The word *opsis* was later used by Aristotle to denote the visual dimension of tragedy in performance. Here it suggests a metatheatrical awareness, on Sophocles' part, of the Messenger's role as the reporter of off-stage events. This in turn invites the audience to reflect upon ways in which the literal visualizations of drama may comment on the larger themes of sight and insight that pervade this particular play.

We hear first of the death of Jokasta, who hangs herself at her bridal bed using her own clothing—a mode of suicide characteristic of women (as opposed to the more manly sword). This is followed by the horrific narrative of Oidipous' self-blinding. This act is not an admission of guilt for the deeds that he did, after all, perform unknowingly. But it is an acknowledgment of horror, shame and pollution. It serves as a powerful way of fulfilling his immediate desire, on discovering the truth, to be cut off from the light of day (1182-51; cf. 1412). Such a desire makes complete sense in view of the many symbolic associations of light—whose god is, of course, Apollo.

Light represents truth, but the truth is intolerable to Oidipous; it represents reason, but reason has failed him; it represents purity, so he can have no contact with it; it represents life, so blinding is a symbolic death. The symbolic equation with death makes blinding in a sense a proper punishment for murder. It is also an expression of intense shame, since shame is often located in the power of seeing and being seen (see 1384-5 with note). The association of Oidipous' shame with vision—both his own and that of others—has been prepared throughout the play (e.g. 792-3, 824, 830-33), and shame plays a central role in his own explanation for his self-blinding (1270-74, 1337-8, 1371-85).

Besides these general associations, Oidipous' deed can also be seen as an appropriate response to his particular offences. The messenger's language suggests that the self-blinding is a symbolic reenactment of—and hence repayment for—those transgressions. When he speaks of "the mingled evils of a man and wife" (1281), he employs a common Greek expression for sexual intercourse, thus equating Oidipous' and Jokasta's present sufferings with their transgressive sexual encounters. In his narrative, Oidipous breaks forcibly into the house and the inner chamber—the realm of women and reproductive sexuality—and stabs his eyes, using the same verb (*paiō* 1252, 1269, 1332) employed earlier for his striking of Laios' driver (807). By removing the pins from Jokasta's clothing as she lies there (1266-9), he effectively undresses her, as if for sexual penetration, an act for which the stabbing of his own eyes is a symbolic substitute. Since the eyes are commonly seen in Greek texts as the seat of eroticism (see e.g. *Ant.* 795-7), self-blinding can be viewed as a punishment for casting one's eyes on an improper erotic object, or even as a form of symbolic castration. (In the Greek mythic tradition, blinding is often a punishment for sexual transgressions.) At the same time, the blood streaming from Oidipous' eye-sockets is in a sense the repayment of "blood for blood" required by Apollo for Laios' death (100). This "bloody hail" (1277-9) also provides an image of perverted fertility which further evokes both the incest (1246, 1257), the plague (25-7, 171-3), and the "storm" of blood afflicting Thebes (22-4, 101).

But if blood must be paid with blood, why does Oidipous not literally kill himself, as Jokasta does? This might seem the only punishment commensurate with the horror of Oidipous' unwitting deeds. And his parting words before he blinds himself, together with other hints in the text, may have led the audience to expect that this was indeed what he would do (see 1183 and 1235 with notes). Self-blinding might seem like a lesser self-punishment than suicide. But as we have seen, it serves many dramatic and symbolic purposes, which make it in many ways a more pointed culmination than death to the central themes of the play, especially the pervasive themes of sight and blindness, light and dark, knowledge and ignorance. Oidipous' desire is not for death as such, but to be cut off from the human contact provided by the senses (1386-90, 1436-7). In an important sense blindness achieves this more than suicide could do, since even in the underworld the shades of the dead can "see" and "address" each other (1371-4), in contrast to the total isolation that Oidipous desires. The chorus declare that self-blinding is a fate worse than death (1367-8), and Oidipous indicates the same thing when he declare that hanging (Jokasta's mode of death) is too good for him (1373-4), implying that to live with the truth is a greater punishment than death would be. Sophocles gives these assertions credibility in part by emphasizing the ghastliness of the deed with exceptionally graphic language (1275-9), and in part through the horrified reaction of others (1298-1307).

The self-blinding is also, in its own way, a heroic action reaffirming the autonomy and decisiveness that originally made Oidipous great. As an active deed of self-assertion, it forms a contrast both with the evils that he previously committed in total ignorance, and with the curse that he unwittingly brought down on his own head (cf. 1230). It is also in marked contrast to the kind of passive despair shown sometimes by other crushed characters, such as Kreon at the end of *Antigone*. Oidipous is great even in defeat. In an important sense, he is now even greater than he was at the outset with his external trappings of power. The strength and clarity of his intellect remain undiminished, as demonstrated by his lucid and logical defense of his self-blinding (1369-90). In addition, he has shown the ability to bear up under extreme suffering, and acquired a new level of self-knowledge. As with Teiresias, his physical blindness betokens a special insight, into both the exceptional nature of his own life (cf. 1455-7) and the limitations of human understanding generally. Unlike Teiresias, however, Oidipous was not a passive recipient of either blindness or insight as a gift from the gods. Rather, he chose both these things in wilful gestures of struggle and pain. His decision to live on, and endure the truth, exemplifies a different heroic pattern from that of Achilles, who chooses glory over a long life, or Ajax, who chooses suicide over disgrace. The Homeric hero he resembles most closely is Odysseus, who travels the world surviving by his wits and learning from his wanderings, is identified by means of a scar (above, p. 122), and remains alive at the end of his heroic narrative.

When the chorus asks Oidipous what god incited his deed

(1327-8), he replies that it was Apollo who "fulfilled" his sufferings, but his own hand that struck the blow (1330-33). This combination of divine and human factors echoes the messenger's account, with its hints that supernatural forces were at work (1258, 1261). But this does not mean Oidipous considers the blinding to be a divine punishment, or blames Apollo for it. He takes full personal responsibility for his deed. The chorus likewise treat him as a responsible agent who has made a choice, despite Apollo's instigation (1327-8). Both he and they are employing a mode of thought sometimes called "double determination," whereby human character is not clearly separable from divine causation. This means that an act may be viewed as caused on a divine and human level simultaneously, without removing responsibility from humans for actions that they purposefully choose. Like every other action in the play, Oidipous' self-blinding is presented as a plausible human action, with no sense of an externally coercive divine power. At the same time, the fact that the blinding was his own choice does not prevent it being part of the fulfilment of Apollo's curse upon his family (cf. 376-7). As usual, the gods function through—not in opposition to—human feelings and behavior. It is Oidipous' character that drives the plot. But it does so against the background of a framework of divine knowledge that places those actions in a different perspective.

Oidipous' self-blinding, in contrast to suicide, also allows the playwright to create a powerful dramatic symmetry between the opening scene of the play and its close. At the outset Oidipous could see physically, but his intellectual vision, however extraordinary, was limited to the level of normal human understanding. Now he is physically blind, but has gained a more profound level of insight. His re-emergence from the palace as a blind man shows this reversal visually to the audience. The king on whom his people depended, whom they supplicated for salvation, is now their helpless dependant and suppliant (1292-3, 1322-3; cf. 40-51). The declaration "I must rule" (628) has been replaced by "I must obey" (1516). The conspicuous exemplar of human success (cf. 7-8) has become a shocking spectacle paradigmatic of misfortune (1294-7, 1304-7, 1391-3; cf. also 145). He who pitied his people (13) is now pitied by them (1295-7). The "best of mortals" (46) has become "evilest" (1433). The man who travelled the world, both literally and intellectually, on his own initiative, is now led passively by others (1309, 1340-41). The man who solved the riddle of the Sphinx, who appeared at the "noon" of human life walking on two legs and using his staff as a symbol of authority, re-emerges using that same staff as the third "leg" that marks the transience and ultimate helplessness of the human condition.

The entrance of Oidipous' young daughters (1470) evokes the prologue in a particularly poignant fashion, recalling as it does his role as "father" of his Theban "children" (above). That relationship has now been reversed, since he is now a helpless, dependent "child" of the city of Thebes (cf. 1098). But the Theban suppliants are replaced by the offspring of his incestuous marriage. The sick "family" of Thebans has been replaced by the grotesquely pathetic "sick" royal family of Thebes (1480-85, 1496-99). Like most young children in tragedy, the girls do not speak, nor are they named or individuated, but they provide a touching dramatic tableau as they cling to their father. The description of their familial closeness, specifically their intimately shared meals, not only conveys an unusually close relationship between father and daughters, but suggests metaphorically the disruption of proper family boundaries. In classical Athens, girls would not eat at the same table as their father. Food, like sex, is a marker of humanity whose boundaries are established and carefully policed by culture, especially through the control of commensality. Incest is a transgressive form of touching, which is evoked by the language of touching that pervades the description of this family's shared meals (1462-70). Note that it is Oidipous' quasi-transgressive, incestuous closeness to his "dearest" daughters that is emphasized (14-74), as opposed to his relationship to his sons, which does not provide the incestuous frisson of cross-gender intimacy. He tells Kreon to let his two adult sons look after themselves, but to take special care of his vulnerable girl-children, to whom he is especially close (1459-66). The effect is further enhanced by the disastrous effects of his behavior on his daughters' marriage prospects (1466-1502).

Kreon's appearance in the final scene, just at the moment when he is needed, provides us with yet another echo, and reversal, of the play's opening (1416; cf. 78-9). The man who sent his brother-in-law on missions as his lieutenant is now subject to that lieutenant's authority; the imperious king must beg favors from someone he previously insulted (compare 1522 with 14). Oidipous beseeches Kreon to kill him or send him into exile (1410-12)—the two possible punishments proposed by the oracle for Laios' killer (100, 308-9, 657-8, 669-70). But exile is what he really wants (1436-7, 1518; cf. 1340-41). As we have seen (above, p. 101), this was the standard Athenian penalty for unintentional homicide. But Oidipous' case is different from that of any other killer. He begs for exile not simply because he killed a man—intentionally or otherwise—but because of the unparalleled pollution caused by his combined parricide and incest (1409-15). At the same time, exile is a fitting fulfilment of his parents' abortive attempt to "throw him out" of Thebes in his infancy (1451-4; compare 1436 with 718).

In most cases of pollution, some kind of ritual purification is possible. But Oidipous' transgressions lie beyond the realm of normal human experience. Unspeakable deeds bring exceptional pollution, and that pollution is infectious. It is true that Oidipous says no one else can be affected (1413-5). But this is a figure of speech, a rhetorical way of expressing the uniqueness of his case. (For this awareness of his own uniqueness compare 1455-7.) He must be expelled from Thebes not simply as a killer, but as the person whose presence has been causing the plague. Thus Kreon says that his very presence outside the house is polluting the sun and the whole of the natural world (1424-31). These words recall a form of oath in which it was prayed that if a man swore falsely, neither earth, nor sea, nor air might tolerate the presence of his corpse. They also evoke the requirements of successful agriculture (earth, rain and sunlight), thus recalling the blight that Oidipous' presence has brought upon Thebes' fertility. His role has therefore often been likened to that of the *pharmakos* or scapegoat—a socially contemptible person who is first fed and cared for royally, then ritually burdened with the evils of the city and expelled from it as a form of purification, especially in times of crisis, including plagues. In some myths, the king is himself the outcast. The same pattern is suggested by his rhetorical declaration at the end of the play that no one can bear his evils but himself (1414-15).

Yet there are also important differences between Oidipous' story and the practice of scapegoating—most notably the fact that he himself performed the deeds polluting the city, and he is not expelled from the city at the end of the play. His case is so extraordinary that, rather than exiling him right away, Kreon wants to consult the Delphic oracle again to find out what to do (1438-9). As the new ruler of Thebes, it is now Kreon's responsibility to send such emissaries, as Oidipous formerly sent him. He also takes on Oidipous' paternal role from the prologue, as is shown most clearly by Oidipous' request that he serve as "father" to Oidipous' children (1503-7).[5] Kreon never explicitly agrees to this request, but he will now be the girls' guardian in any case, as their uncle and the new head of the patriarchal family.[6] But although the two men's situations have been reversed,

5 At 1505 Oidipous actually addresses Kreon as "father," making the role-reversal still more pointed. But the text translated here is based on a conjecture.

6 If we are right in thinking this play followed the production of *Antigone* by a number of years, then we may reasonably assume that Sophocles expects us to remember that Kreon actually killed Antigone in the play named for her.

there is little change in their characters. Kreon continues to advocate concealment (1424-31; cf. 91-2) and avoid personal responsibility (1438-43, 1518-20). Oidipous, by contrast, displays his misery openly, and advocates swift decisive action. As he says, it seems quite obvious that he should leave Thebes immediately (1440-43). Mythically, this is the eventual outcome (Oidipous is right). But his desire is thwarted by the cautious Kreon, effectively underlining Oidipous' loss of power, his helplessness and frustration. Oidipous, on the other hand, remains remarkably vigorous, assertive and willful. Despite his blindness, which renders him physically helpless, and the degradation of his polluted state, he continues to give orders to Kreon and others, to plan for the future, to take care of others, and to rebuff the chorus' opinions (1340-41, 1369-70, 1446-54, 1459-67, 1503-7). In all these ways he resembles his old self (compare 1446 with 252, 1522-3 with 14). To the end, he resists Kreon's orders and tries to set his own conditions for obeying (1517, 1521-2). In the very last words of the play, Kreon must tell him not to try to be master still (1523-4).[7] Instead of the exile he desires, Oidipous is led into the house, in a passage that reverses the trajectory of his initial kingly emergence from that house, symbolically emasculating him and forcing him to face the appalling implications of his domestic life.

The indeterminacy of this ending replicates the uncertainty of human life that has been such a central theme of the play. Oidipous must live as Jokasta recommended, subject to the whims of Fortune. But he will do so henceforth as a survivor of the worst that Fortune can do to a man, and with an extraordinary level of self-knowledge. The nature of that knowledge—a newfound understanding of his place in the larger divinely-ordered pattern of events—is indicated by his certainty that he is destined for a special death (1455-7). Sophocles would complete the pattern of Oidipous' remarkable life by dramatizing that death in his last play, decades later.

---

7   Many editors think that the final choral tag is spurious. But even if it is authentic, Kreon gets the last word of any of the individual characters.

Suggestions for Further Reading

This is only a tiny sample of the innumerable works devoted to Greek tragedy, Sophocles and *King Oidipous*. It includes works cited by author and date in the text, together with others chosen for their interest and accessibility to the English-speaking reader.

CULTURAL AND RELIGIOUS BACKGROUND

Burkert, W. *Greek Religion* (Eng. trans. Cambridge, Mass. 1985) [invaluable concise survey of the gods and their cults]

Buxton, Richard. *Imaginary Greece: The Contexts of Mythology* (Cambridge 1994) [the cultural contexts of myth-telling]

Ehrenberg, V. *From Solon to Socrates* (2nd ed. London 1973) [history of the sixth and fifth centuries with a cultural emphasis]

Fantham, E., H. Foley, N. Kampen, S. Pomeroy and A. Shapiro (edd.). *Women in the Classical World* (Oxford 1994)

Gantz, Timothy. *Early Greek Myth: A Guide to Literary and Artistic Sources* (Johns Hopkins UP 1993) [indispensable for the serious study of Greek myth]

Howatson, M.C. (ed.). *The Concise Oxford Companion to Classical Literature* (Oxford 1993) [a handy reference for looking up names in myth, history etc.]

Lloyd-Jones, H. *The Justice of Zeus* (2nd ed. Berkeley and Los Angeles 1983)

Parker, Robert. *Miasma: Pollution and Purification in Greek Religion* (Oxford 1983)

Tyrrell, William Blake and Frieda S. Brown. *Athenian Myths and Institutions* (Oxford 1991) [the uses of myth in Athenian culture]

BOOKS ON ANCIENT GREEK TRAGEDY

Buxton, R.G.A. *Persuasion in Greek Tragedy* (Cambridge 1982) [a useful account of an important aspect of drama]

Csapo, Eric and Slater, William J. *The Context of Ancient Drama* (Ann Arbor 1995) [surveys all the evidence for the ancient theater and production]

Foley, Helene. *Female Acts in Greek Tragedy* (Princeton 2001) [examines problems of female agency in tragedy, in the context of Athenian gender norms]

Goldhill, S. *Reading Greek Tragedy* (Cambridge 1986) [an introduction from the perspective of recent critical theory]

Jones, John. *On Aristotle and Greek Tragedy* (London 1962) [challenges the view that character is central to Greek tragedy]

Kitto, H.D.F. *Greek Tragedy* (3rd ed. London 1961) [a still valuable introduction]

Lesky, A. *Greek Tragic Poetry* (Eng. trans. New Haven 1983) [a thorough survey of tragedy and scholarship]

McClure, Laura. *Spoken like a Woman: Speech and Gender in Athenian Drama* (Princeton 1999)

Rehm, Rush. *Greek Tragic Theater* (London 1992) [a good introduction from the perspective of performance]

———. *Marriage to Death* (Princeton 1994) [a detailed exploration of an important complex of ideas]

Taplin, O. *Greek Tragedy in Action* (London 1978) [a fine introduction to tragedy in performance]

Vernant, Jean-Pierre and Pierre Vidal-Naquet. *Myth and Tragedy in Ancient Greece*, trans. Janet Lloyd (New York 1988) [influential structuralist interpretation]

Vickers, B. *Towards Greek Tragedy* (London 1973) [makes good use of mythic, social and religious background]

Wiles, David. *Tragedy in Athens: Performance Space and Theatrical Meaning* (Cambridge 1997)

———. *Greek Theatre Performance: An Introduction* (Cambridge 2000)

Williams, Bernard. *Shame and Necessity* (Berkeley and Los Angeles 1993) [an important study of Greek values surrounding agency and responsibility]

Winkler, J. and F. Zeitlin (edd.) *Nothing to Do with Dionysos?* (Princeton 1990) [places Athenian drama in its political context]

Wohl, Victoria. *Intimate Commerce: Exchange, Gender, and Subjectivity in Greek Tragedy* (Austin 1998) [a contemporary feminist reading]

BOOKS ON SOPHOCLES
(all include some discussion of one or more of the Theban plays)

Blundell, M.W. *Helping Friends and Harming Enemies: A Study in Sophocles and Greek Ethics* (Cambridge 1989) [discusses Sophocles in the context of Greek popular morality]

Bowra, C.M. *Sophoclean Tragedy* (Oxford 1944) [old-fashioned but still valuable for its learning]

Ehrenberg, Victor. *Sophocles and Pericles* (Oxford 1954) [relates Sophocles' plays to the political context of his time]

Gardiner: C.P. *The Sophoclean Chorus: A Study of Character and Function* (Iowa City 1987) [looks at the chorus as a character]

Gellie, G.H. *Sophocles: A Reading* (Melbourne 1972) [an accessible introduction]

Kirkwood, G.M. *A Study of Sophoclean Drama* (Ithaca 1958) [good on character and aspects of dramatic technique]

Knox, B.M.W. *The Heroic Temper* (Berkeley 1964) [an influential and readable account of the Sophoclean 'hero']

Ormand, Kirk. *Exchange and the Maiden: Marriage in Sophoclean Tragedy* (Texas 1999) [explores ways in which the plays problematize the Greek ideology of marriage]

Reinhardt, K. *Sophocles* (English trans. Oxford 1979) [demanding but influential]

Scodel, R. *Sophocles* (Boston 1984) [a stimulating introduction]

Seale, D. *Vision and Stagecraft in Sophocles* (London 1982) [explores visual aspects and imagery of sight]

Segal, C.P. *Tragedy and Civilization: An Interpretation of Sophocles* (Cambridge, Mass. 1981) [a detailed structuralist account]

------------. *Sophocles' Tragic World: Divinity, Nature, Society* (Harvard 1995) [a collection of the author's essays, many on *OT*]

Waldock, A.J.A. *Sophocles the Dramatist* (Cambridge 1951) [refreshingly iconoclastic, if often wrong-headed]

Webster, T.B.L. *An Introduction to Sophocles* (Oxford 1936) [old-fashioned but still useful, especially on Sophocles' life]

Whitman, C.H. *Sophocles, A Study in Heroic Humanism* (Cambridge, Mass. 1951) [dated but often stimulating]

Winnington-Ingram, R.P. *Sophocles: An Interpretation* (Cambridge 1980) [an outstanding study by a sensitive scholar]

WORKS ON THE THEBAN PLAYS, ESP. *KING OIDIPOUS*

Ahl, Frederick. *Sophocles' Oedipus: Evidence and Self-Contradiction* (Ithaca, NY 1991) [revives the provocative view that Oedipus did *not* kill his father or marry his mother]

Burkert, Walter. *Oedipus, Oracles, and Meaning* (Toronto 1991) [a brief and readable introductory essay]

Bushnell, Rebecca W. *Prophesying Tragedy: Sign and Voice in Sophocles' Theban Plays* (Ithaca, NY 1988) [a semiotic interpretation using the theme of prophecy]

Cameron, Alister. *The Identity of Oedipus the King* (New York 1968) [a straightforward introduction for the general reader]

Dodds, E.R. 'On misunderstanding the *Oedipus Rex*,' *Greece and Rome* 13 (1966) 37-49; reprinted in E.R. Dodds, *The Ancient Concept of Progress* (Oxford 1973) and E. Segal (ed.) *Greek Tragedy* (New York 1983) [a landmark essay still useful on guilt and pollution]

Edmunds, L. and A. Dundes (edd.). *Oedipus: A Folklore Casebook* (New York 1983) [a wealth of parallels to the Oidipous story from other cultures]

Griffith, R. Drew *The Theatre of Apollo: Divine Justice and Sophocles' Oedipus the King* (McGill-Queens UP 1996) [perverse but sometimes insightful]

Knox, Bernard. *Oedipus at Thebes: Sophocles' Tragic Hero and his Time* (2nd. Ed. New Haven 1998) [a justly famous study identifying Oedipus with Athens]

O'Brien, M.J. (ed.). *Twentieth-Century Interpretations of Oedipus Rex* (Englewood Cliffs, NJ 1968)

Pucci, Pietro, *Oedipus and the Fabrication of the Father: Oedipus Tyrannus in Modern Criticism and Philosophy* (Baltimore 1992)

Segal, Charles. *Oedipus Tyrannus: Tragic Heroism and the Limits of Knowledge* (2nd. edn. Oxford 2001) [an accessible introduction for the general reader]

Van Nortwick, T. *Oedipus: The Meaning of a Masculine Life* (University of Oklahoma Press 1998) [Oidipous as a paradigm for masculine psychological development]